Historic
INNS
AND
TAVERNS
of Wales and
the Marches

PAUL R. DAVIS

ALAN SUTTON

To T.L., J.M., K.S. and S.J. for indirect help along the way

First published in the United Kingdom in 1993 by
Alan Sutton Publishing Limited · Phoenix Mill · Far Thrupp · Stroud · Gloucestershire

First published in the United States of America in 1993
Alan Sutton Publishing Inc · 83 Washington Street · Dover · NH 03820

British Library Cataloguing in Publication Data

Davis, Paul R.
Historic Inns of Wales and the Marches
I. Title
647. 94429
ISBN 0–7509–0202–7

Library of Congress Cataloging in Publication Data applied for

Typeset in Sabon 11/14
Typesetting and origination by
Alan Sutton Publishing Limited.
Printed in Great Britain by
The Bath Press, Avon

CONTENTS

The gazetteer has been arranged for the sake of convenience into six geographic areas, and the individual entries listed alphabetically after the village or town name. Directions on how to reach the various pubs are given at the end of each entry, together with basic details of amenities. The opening hours are correct at the time of writing, and since Sunday hours are generally standard (12–3 p.m., 7–10.30 p.m.) they have not been indicated, unless different.

Following each section there is an end list of additional pubs and inns which were built before 1750, or contain some early work; the lists are by no means complete, and any additions or corrections would be most welcome.

INTRODUCTION

'There is nothing which has yet been contrived by man, by which so much happiness is produced as by a good tavern or inn'
— Samuel Johnson (1709–84)

'The innkeepers are insolent, the hostlers are sulky, the chambermaids are pert, and the waiters are impertinent; the meat is tough, the wine is foul, the beer is hard and the sheets wet; the linen is dirty, and the knives are never clean'
— Viscount Torrington (1742–1813)

The above quotes serve to highlight the extreme views people have voiced over the centuries about inns, pubs and taverns: loved by the inveterate customer, loathed by the puritanical teetotaller. But there is no doubt that this ancient establishment has always played an important role in the social life of a town or village.

How far back do we go in search of the 'historic' inn? To the crumbling foundations unearthed by archaeologists at Roman sites, some of which were undoubtedly the *tavernae* frequented by off-duty imperial troops? Or to the rough hostelries familiar to Chaucer and Shakespeare, which by today have been modernized almost out of recognition? Is it the age of a building which matters, or the length of time it has been used as an inn? Are pubs really as old as some stories claim, and what architectural merits, if any, do they possess? Some of these questions will be answered in the following pages, for this book is concerned not so much with the variety of beer on tap nor the mouthwatering diversity of the menu, but rather the buildings themselves. More than anything, this is a guide to vernacular architecture, the buildings raised using traditional methods by yeomen, merchants and wealthy landowners, from the Middle Ages to the Industrial Revolution. Unless the reader is fortunate enough to live in a sixteenth- or seventeenth-century house, then an old pub or inn offers an uncommon opportunity to see the inside of such a building. Although the majority of interiors have been extensively modernized, most publicans appreciate the intrinsic value of their property, and are at pains to re-create or conserve the 'Olde Worlde' environs. The interior of a brass-festooned and black-beamed pub, warmed by a crackling log fire, conjures an appealing image of a sedate, rustic time in days gone by, with all the convenience of the twentieth century and without the discomforts and harsh realities of life in the not so distant past.

The terms inn, tavern and alehouse are rarely used today with the same strictness as in older times, and indeed you will be hard pressed to find an 'alehouse' in any modern town or city. An inn primarily offered accommodation and food to the wayfarer, a role today largely taken over by guest-houses and hotels. In both taverns and alehouses the main function was the provision of drink, though the tavern was for the more discerning customer where food and wine was consumed. The town and village locals of the twentieth century therefore trace their origins back to the old alehouse. 'The ancient, true and proper use of inns, alehouses and victualling houses was for the receipt, relief and lodging of wayfarers . . . and not for the entertainment and harbouring of lewd and idle people' proclaimed a Parliamentary Act of 1604.

The very image of an inn or pub nestling alongside the church by the green is essentially an English one, since the town was a product of the feudal society introduced into Wales by the Normans. For most of the Middle Ages Welsh settlement was confined to scattered farmsteads, some grouped in the vicinity of native churches. No pub would have been commercially viable in such locations, and any ale would have been brewed by the farmer's wife for the family's own consumption, or for some neighbourly trade. In the towns and trading centres established by the English under the protective wing of mighty castles there was far greater opportunity for business. But any growth was limited to one important factor – the availability of customers. Even into the eighteenth century people only travelled by necessity, and the road network was so bad that travel itself was an ordeal rather than a pleasure. During the Middle Ages only kings, wealthy landowners, drovers and pilgrims braved the perils of the open road; apart from the threat of cut-throats, highwaymen and wild animals there was the road itself to be endured. 'What am I to say of the roads in this country . . . mere rocky lanes full of hugeous stones as big as one's horses, and abominable holes . . . without either direction posts or mile stones', and this was in 1772!

The monasteries which attracted the prayers and coins of devout pilgrims also set up hostelries for their benefit, but none now survive in Wales. Similarly the tales that certain inns were built to house workmen constructing an adjacent church (see p. 81) may well be true in theory, but cannot be borne out by architectural evidence – too often the church is older than the inn, not the other way around! Henry VIII closed down the monasteries between 1536 and 1540, and the various estates were sold off to wealthy landowners to fill the royal coffers. A well-run monastic inn became a well-run secular one; but even though the collapse of feudalism meant that fewer people were tied to the land and so could move about the country more freely, there was still the basic problem of the roads. In 1555 Parliament passed an act enabling parish councils to conscript labour to help repair the local roads, but this was rarely enforced, and most men viewed roadwork days as time off. The first significant step in improving travel came in 1663, when the first turnpike trust was established in Hertfordshire. A group of investors undertook to maintain a stretch of the county road, and regain their capital by charging a toll on all users. The idea was slow to catch on at first, and in rural Wales the improvements were not felt until the second half of the eighteenth century. Some of the trusts, however, had insufficient funds or motivation to tackle the difficult terrain of upland Wales, and the single most important advance in travel came about in 1815–30, when Thomas Telford constructed the Shrewsbury to Holyhead road and improved stretches of the coastal route between Bangor and Chester.

Even with better roads it could still take many days to complete a long journey, and so inns and hostelries were essential establishments along the main routes. In 1750 the average coach speed was 7 mph, and a trip from Shrewsbury to London could take up to four days! The era of the horse and coach reached its peak between 1780 and 1830, and thereafter declined in favour of the railway. The inns built during this period have less in common with earlier buildings, since they were designed solely with guest accommodation in mind and contained as many small rooms as possible under one roof. The increasing number of artists and travelogue writers who visited Wales from the eighteenth century onwards, in search of the 'Romantic' landscape, led to many small farms and houses opening their doors as pubs and inns. The comments and often effusive descriptions provided by these early tourists give us a tolerably accurate picture of the rural inn, and some examples will be found in the following pages.

Many towns and villages had an excessive number of public houses, far more than one would think the population could support. Caernarfon had fifty, Clun sixteen, Hay forty-six, and Denbigh over sixty. Only a fraction of these remain, but since most were little more than the front room of a house it is understandable that when trade declined the change back into a shop or residence was accomplished with relative ease. Most rural inns developed from a purely domestic building, only to revert to its original role in later years. Today the pressure to succeed in business is greater than ever. A recent survey has shown that there are more than 150 pubs for sale in Dyfed alone, and while researching this book dozens of pubs earmarked for inclusion were visitd, only to be found closed and shuttered. Sadder still are the ones which were visited, described and illustrated, only to be withdrawn before publication because they had closed in the meantime. They will surely open their doors again – but as drinking places, or desirable period homes?

ARCHITECTURAL INTRODUCTION

If the geographic limits of this book were to be extended to incorporate the rest of England, then examples would be included of the large, purpose-built inns and hostelries of the late Middle Ages. The George (Dorchester-on-Thames), the New Inn (Gloucester), the King's Head (Aylesbury) and the George (Norton St Philip) are classic examples of the inns frequented by pilgrims and other hardy medieval travellers. The buildings contain numerous rooms, overlooking a rear courtyard with stables for accommodating the horses. Similar inns survive in the more important pilgrimage centres, such as Canterbury, Walsingham and Glastonbury, but in Wales and the Marches they invariably date from after the seventeenth century, when the more settled conditions and improving road network made travel less of an ordeal. Few town inns in the rural areas of Wales could have accommodated more than half a dozen travellers at any one time, though with several hostelries in each place this was not such a problem as it might seem. Furthermore, the concepts of privacy and comfort, which we take for granted today, were enjoyed only by the wealthy few. A room would probably have accommodated several guests at one time. Even in a large inn such as the Skirrid (p. 42) there are no more than eight rooms in the building, including the kitchen, with attic space for servants' quarters. Other inns had fewer rooms, and even if today light partitions split up the interior into numerous bedrooms and corridors, a close examination of the building will reveal that this was not the original plan. Evidently the 'purpose-built' inn reached Wales only in the last 300 years, when there was an increasing need for such an establishment.

As far as architecture is concerned, all but a few of the historic pubs included in this book are virtually indistinguishable from the thousands of farmhouses and cottages scattered through the land. The only obvious difference would have been a sign displaying the name and function of the building. The public drinking area (the bar, after all, is a Victorian invention) would have been located in the main room of the house, the hall, invariably the largest, and sometimes the only room with any heating. The inglenooks beloved of pub guides once formed the heart of the house, where the family and guests would huddle together for warmth and light. Such grand fireplaces still form the main attraction in renovated pubs, though it is usually a more energy efficient gas or coal fire which actually provides the heat.

Since there is little structural difference between a seventeenth-century house and a seventeenth-century pub, it is essential to outline the development of domestic architecture from the Middle Ages to the Industrial Revolution. But before moving on it is worth examining two popular pub traditions. The first is the widespread belief that the hefty timbers in a roof and ceiling came from a ship. In areas close to a port, or where driftwood from a wreck could be easily obtained, such tales may well be true. But what of pubs 30 miles or more inland? Why should anyone go to the trouble of dragging great beams across country, when a forest of oaks may be at hand? One theory is that the persistent belief arose from the use of the term 'ship's timber' to describe a certain quality of wood, and the holes and slots pointed out on some beams as evidence of re-use are usually the mortice holes of a dismantled partition. The second tradition is one that many landlords fiercely defend, and which anyone would be ill-advised to ridicule. This is the highly prized title of oldest pub or inn in Britain. There are so many contenders for this race, but few pass the final hurdle. Here in Wales dozens of establishments boast a venerable age – the Skirrid is the best known – but the claims are rarely backed up by architectural evidence. Although documents refer to an inn at Llanfihangel Crucorney in the twelfth century, it was certainly not the Skirrid as claimed, since this building is no older than the seventeenth century. By contrast, the Priory Inn (p. 16) and Old Cross Keys (p. 19) are genuine medieval buildings dating from the thirteenth and fourteenth centuries, but neither were built originally as pubs, and the Priory has been in commercial use for only a few years. If the author is forced to award the accolade of 'oldest pub' to the entries in this book, and if the decisive category is architectural age rather than commercial usage, then the first prize should be awarded jointly to the Priory Inn (p. 16), Old Cross Keys (p. 19) and the Nag's Head (p. 59). All three are comparatively recent pubs, but incorporate masonry of thirteenth- and fourteenth-century date. Second place goes to the Old Mason's Arms (p. 35) which may also be fourteenth century, and the fifteenth-century Black Swan (p. 96) runs a close third. The other pubs built before 1500 included here are Baron's Court (p. 61), the Tram Inn (p. 83), the Red Lion (p. 122), and the King's Head (p. 136).

MEDIEVAL HOUSES

Throughout the Middle Ages and into the early post-Reformation period the majority of houses were built of two materials, or combinations of both – wood and stone. Their distribution is confined to the availability of the material, and so in mountainous Wales stone buildings predominate. Wood is used only for door and window frames, some internal partitions and roof supports. As one travels further east the grey stone houses make way for the familiar and picturesque timber-framed buildings, where the only obvious masonry is usually the chimney-stack. Materials apart, the major difference between the two types of building is that stone houses were built *in situ*, while the component parts of a half-timbered structure would be shaped and assembled at the carpenter's yard, before being moved and re-erected at its designated site.

It has been said that the greater the age of a building, the more likely it is to have been constructed by someone of a high social standing. Only the more substantial buildings survive the centuries. During the Middle Ages 'home' for the vast majority of people consisted of a hall – a long, high room open to the roof, and heated by a fire burning on a hearth in the middle of the floor. Of course the scale and grandeur of the hall depended on the wealth of the occupant; who can fail to be impressed by the cavernous interiors of the great halls at Stokesay Castle, Tretower Court, Berkeley Castle or Penshurst Place? The atmosphere would have been just as bad as in a poorer yeoman's house, but at least the higher roofs allowed most of the smoke from the hearth to rise!

A typical medieval house consisted of a central hall flanked at either end by a set of rooms, usually of two storeys. At the lower, or entry, end of the hall were service rooms such as stores, pantry and buttery. Separating these from the hall itself was an entrance walkway between opposing doorways, the cross-passage. Sometimes the passage was partitioned off from the hall, but more often it was open, perhaps with a movable screen to control excessive draughts. The open hearth stood near the middle of the floor, and a vent or louvre in the roof above enabled the smoke to escape. Glass was such an expensive commodity that for centuries windows were generally unglazed and positioned on each side of the house, so that the shutters could be opened for light on the side sheltered from the wind. The far end of the hall was reserved for the high table, usually set on a raised platform, the dais, and here the family would sit at mealtimes. A door beside the dais led through to the solar, or private chambers. The separate elements of the hall clearly had a hierarchical role to play, emphasizing the social standing of the occupants, just as architectural embellishments did in houses of the Renaissance.

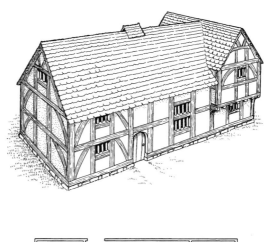

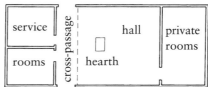

A typical medieval house

In towns and cities space was generally at a premium, and this led to certain modifications in the plan. Houses were built on narrow plots running back from the street, with oversailing upper floors stacked precariously on top of each other. The open hall was still a feature of urban buildings, though it was generally smaller than its rural counterpart, and located to the rear of a street-front shop or workroom. In stone houses the hall was often located on the first floor with an enclosed fireplace and chimney; but such features did not become commonplace until the sixteenth century, and houses still depended on an open hearth for warmth. Few hall-houses remain in their original state, as over the years changing tastes affected the layout and arrangement of the interior. While the hall remained the most important room, it gradually began to be reduced in size and grandeur until today the term is used almost derisively to refer to the little passageway at the front door.

POST-MEDIEVAL HOUSES

The more settled years of the Tudor dynasty in England and Wales brought about significant changes in the development of house and home. Economic conditions in the sixteenth century enabled landowners living on fixed tenures

Much Dewchurch, the Black Swan: cutaway reconstruction showing the medieval hall in its original form. The upper part of the cruck trusses and the form of the gallery are conjectural, but other details can be inferred from surviving features. The room on the right of the hall is here assumed to have existed, but no evidence for this now remains. Compare with the drawing on p. 98 which shows the inn after the seventeenth-century rebuilding

to gain from the rising prices of their produce, without having to pay higher rents. More land was developed to achieve bigger surpluses and greater profits, and the money gained was invested in more durable houses with a greater emphasis on domestic comfort than before. In such a competitive market, it was usually those of a higher standing with ready cash and initiative who benefited the most. This 'Great Rebuilding' reached a peak in the period between the Act of Union (1536) and the Civil War (1640), and studies have shown that it spread like a wave from east to west, reaching parts of west Wales as late as the nineteenth century. The majority of houses dating from before 1600 are to be found east of a line drawn between Rhyl on the north coast and Newport in the south; while another line between Conwy and Swansea roughly demarcates the extent of most pre-1700 houses. The old counties of Cardigan and Carmarthenshire have few early buildings when compared to the rich vernacular heritage of Glamorgan, for instance. This helps to explain the gaps on the gazetteer maps: where there are few old houses there are likely to be fewer old pubs!

The new buildings of the post-medieval period were built on two or more floors throughout, and while the hall remained the most important room it no longer had the space and grandeur of its medieval predecessor. Existing halls were modified to serve the increasingly sophisticated requirements of the occupants; an upper floor was inserted into the roof area, and the open hearth therefore had to be replaced by a brick or stone fireplace. The Tram Inn (p. 83), Red Lion (p. 122) and Black Swan (p. 96) are examples of modified timber-framed halls, and the smoke blackened roof truss obscured by the attic in the Tram is a classic indication of its open hall origin. Such alterations greatly increased the accommodation and provided more privacy than before. The smaller rooms may have been just as dark and draughty, but at least the inhabitants no longer had to put up with the smoke and soot from an open hearth. Rather surprisingly, not everyone was overwhelmed by the changes. In 1632 the mathematician Edward Howes commented: 'I like well the old English . . . building where the room is large and the chimney or hearth in the middle. Certainly thereby ill vapour and gnats are kept out, less fuel will serve the turn, and men had then more lusty and able bodies than they have now.' Anyone who has emerged coughing from the re-created halls at the St Fagans Folk Museum, and Avoncroft Museum of Buildings, may not be inclined to agree with Mr Howes.

In the Marches and parts of eastern Wales the converted hall is fairly widespread, but elsewhere in the country the post-medieval storeyed house predominates. Houses with more than one floor and an enclosed fire may well have spread out from towns and cities, where lack of space and stringent fire regulations necessitated such developments from an early time. These buildings have been grouped into various categories by the relative positions of the entrance and the main fireplace in the hall; and there are distinct regional preferences for certain plans.

The most common type of all (since it formed the basic plan of eighteenth-

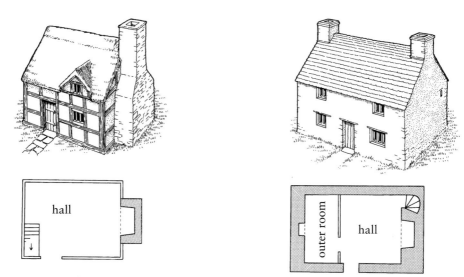

Direct-entry houses: (left) the hall is the only ground-floor room; (right) with an outer room on the entry side

and nineteenth-century cottages) is the end-chimney direct-entry house, where the main fireplace is positioned in the gable furthest from the entrance, which leads straight into the hall. In small houses the hall may be the only ground-floor room but more often there is another room on the entry (or 'outer') side of the hall, as at the Lough Pool (p. 107), the Sun (p. 152) and the Penlan (p. 170). In some larger buildings, for example the Talbot (p. 152), there is an

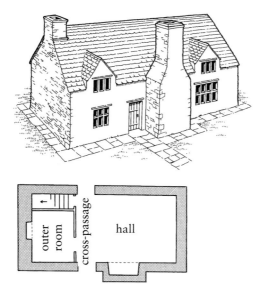

A lateral chimney house

additional 'inner' room beyond the hall, so that the plan reflects the basic arrangements of the medieval house. Although the direct-entry house can be found throughout the country, the main concentration of sixteenth- and seventeenth-century examples occurs in north-west and south-east Wales.

Some buildings of this plan have the main fireplace in the side wall, rather than the gable, and are called lateral chimney houses. This is probably the earliest type of enclosed fireplace, for it appears in late-medieval halls such as Baron's Court (p. 61) and the Bell Inn (p. 33), and also in early storeyed houses, including the King's Head (p. 14), the Robin Hood (p. 58), the Butcher's Arms (p. 109) and the George and Dragon (p. 162). There is also a tendency for the lateral chimney to appear in buildings of a higher social standing, and both Penllwyn (p. 26) and the Skirrid (p. 42) have huge twin stacks.

A somewhat older house type and one that traces its ancestry directly from the rebuilt medieval hall is the 'chimney-backing-on-the-entry' plan, also more conveniently known as a hearth-passage house. Halls like the Tram Inn had their open hearths replaced with a fireplace and flue which backed on to the cross-passage, so that the hall was entered from 'behind' the fireplace. Again, there is some variation in the number and arrangements of the rooms in a typical hearth-passage house. Larger examples like the Blue Anchor (p. 24),

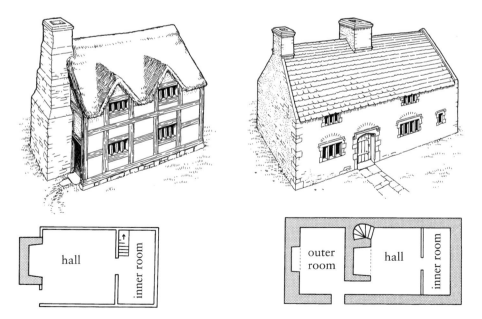

Hearth-passage houses: (left) with hall and inner room; (right) with hall, outer and inner rooms

Cilgerran, the Pendre: this drawing of the hall shows the characteristic feature hearth-passage house, where the main room is entered from 'behind' the fireplace. The beamed ceiling and bay window (on the left) were probably added in the seventeenth century to an earlier open hall

the Star (p. 39), the Royal Oak (p. 52) and the Ship (p. 69) have an outer room, hall and inner room; while the Pandy Inn (p. 80) and White Hart (p. 46) have just a hall and inner room. In contrast the Pendre (p. 3) and the Bush (p. 71) have an outer room and hall, but no inner room. The most famous member of this group is the longhouse, an ancient dwelling where man and beast were accommodated under the same roof. The outer room was used as a cowshed, so that anyone entering the hall had to first pass through the byre. None of the pubs and inns included here appear to have originated as longhouses, although animals are said to have been kept inside the Old Swan (p. 52), the Royal Oak (p. 86) and Oak Inn (p. 119) at times. The hearth-passage type is particularly numerous in the south and east of the country, but noticeably rare in Gwynedd, where the direct-entry plan predominates.

The third main house type is one that can also trace its roots back to the converted hall, but here the fireplace is not built backing on to the entrance but directly opposite it, forming a small lobby alongside. The greatest distribution of the lobby-entry house (sometimes called a baffle-entry) is in the

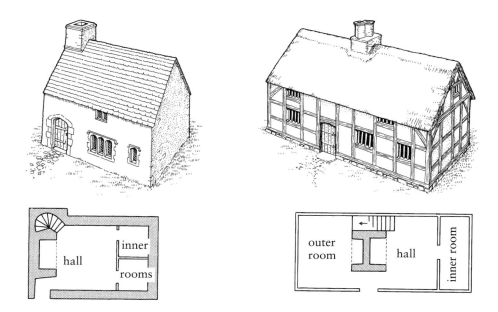

Lobby-entry houses (left) with hall and inner rooms; (right) with hall, inner and outer rooms

Marches and in particular the old county of Montgomeryshire, where the central chimney has back-to-back fireplaces heating the hall and outer room. Classic examples of this type include the Dolfor Inn (p. 118), the Blue Bell (p. 125) and the Star (p. 154). Smaller houses such as the Plough and Harrow (p. 56), the Buck Inn (p. 130) and the Golden Grove (p. 153) have only a hall and inner room.

Even as the new storeyed houses were being built, the first indications of a change in architectural styles began to appear. The ideals of the Renaissance were concerned with the revival of Classical orders, where symmetry, decoration and a certain rigidity of form were the essential ingredients. Although at first confined to the greater houses of the gentry, the new ideas took some time to filter down to the lower-class houses, and local craftsmen still relied on the traditional plans and details. The most obvious change was an increase in external ornamentation; multiple dormers, symmetrically arranged windows, grand entrance porches, heraldic crests, and elaborate timberwork all epitomize the Renaissance houses built before *c.* 1700. During the eighteenth century plans and details were refined even further, giving rise to compact box-like buildings with rows of sash windows; and it was this type of dwelling which replaced the long, low houses of the previous centuries. The

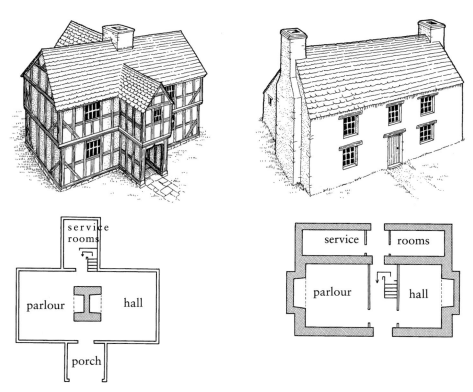

A Renaissance centrally-planned house, before *c*. 1700 (left), and (right) a typical eighteenth-century house

most important change brought about by the Renaissance affected the interior layout. The reduced hall no longer dominated the plan, and the parlour was often the larger and more prestigious room; kitchen and service rooms were banished to the rear of the building. The front entrance generally led to a central corridor or lobby, which separated the ground-floor rooms, and contained the main stair to the upper floors. The advantages of such a centralized plan are obvious; more efficient circulation between rooms and greater privacy for the occupants. At the Skirrid Inn (p. 42), New Inn (p. 68) and Radnorshire Arms (p. 104) the grand staircases are housed in turrets projecting from the back of the building. Much more numerous are the smaller houses like the Swan (p. 7), the Ram (p. 11), the White Hart (p. 12) and the Hundred House (p. 114), where the stairway is contained within the central passage, or is in a rear lean-to.

CONCLUSION

These, then, are the main types of houses built between the sixteenth and nineteenth centuries, and it should be remembered that the plan-types mentioned above relate to the original layout of the building. There are few old houses that have escaped some form of modernization or alteration over the years. Any student of vernacular architecture needs to question whether the features looked at are original, and in the 'right' places. At the Horse and Jockey (p. 67), for instance, there are clear signs that the entrance has been moved no less than three times! Not only the layout but also the internal features can be altered and disguised; the great ceiling beams were often hacked about and plastered over by the Victorians, who disliked the sight of bare wood. The spacious inglenooks were blocked up and replaced with tiny fireplaces in the understandable desire to cut down on heat loss. And yet for many people it is these very features which epitomize the character of an old pub, and which landlords wisely conserve and restore. But in some inns and pubs, centuries-old features are locked away behind papered walls and plastered ceilings, awaiting rediscovery by chance or design.

FURTHER READING

Bruning, T. and Paulin, K., *Historic English Inns* (David and Charles, 1982)

Brunskill, R.W., *Traditional Buildings of Britain* (Gollancz, 1981)

Clark, P., *The English Alehouse* (Longman, 1983)

Dafydd, Myrddin ap, *Welsh Pub Signs* (Gwasg Carreg Gwlach, 1991)

Harris, R., *Discovering timber-framed buildings* (Shire publications, 1978)

Haslam, R., *Powys* (Penguin, 1979 – The Buildings of Britain)

Hubbard, E., *Clwyd* (Penguin, 1986 – The Buildings of Britain)

Hubbard, E. and Pevsner, N., *Cheshire* (Penguin, 1971 – The Buildings of England)

Mercer, E., *English vernacular houses* (HMSO 1975)

Pevsner, N., *Shropshire* (Penguin, 1958 – The Buildings of England)

Pevsner, N., *Herefordshire* (Penguin, 1963 – The Buildings of England)

Raglan, Lord and Fox, Cyril, *Monmouthshire Houses* (Cardiff, 1951–4)

Royal Commission on Ancient and Historical Monuments (Wales), *Glamorgan Inventories,* vol. 3 part 2 (HMSO, 1982), vol. 4 part 2 (HMSO, 1988)

Royal Commission on Ancient and Historical Monuments (England), *Herefordshire Inventories* (HMSO, 1934–6)

Smith, P., *Houses of the Welsh Countryside* (HMSO, 1988)

1. WEST WALES

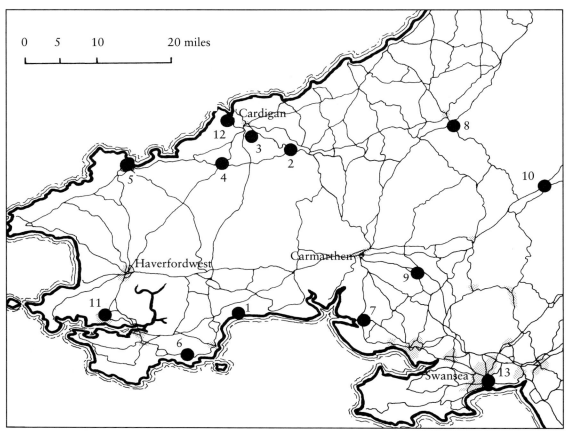

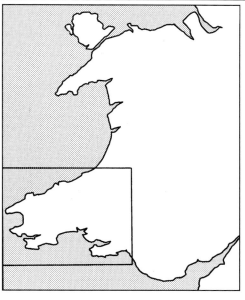

1. Amroth
2. Cenarth
3. Cilgerran
4. Eglwyswrw
5. Fishguard
6. Jameston
7. Kidwelly
8. Lampeter
9. Llanddarog
10. Llandovery
11. Milford Haven
12. St Dogmaels
13. Swansea

New Inn, AMROTH

(SN 173 073)

The New Inn at Amroth stands tall and proud on the seashore, daring the might of the winter storms which sweep this stretch of the Pembrokeshire coast. The huge shingle bank along the front protects the houses and cottages from all but the most voracious tempest, but precautionary sandbags are always at hand. This stone-built inn is said to date from the sixteenth century, but the tall front block with sash windows and a central doorway, looks no earlier than *c.* 1800. Inside there are two stone fireplaces at either end of the long bar, which has been made even longer by the removal of the partitions which formerly divided up the ground floor. At the rear is a separate bar-lounge with a lower ceiling, flagstone floor and a cavernous inglenook honeycombed with nooks and crannies. Some of the openings look like modified ovens, and so this room was very likely a kitchen. All the features look much older than the front wing, however, hinting that this kitchen is, in fact, the remains of an earlier cottage which was incorporated into the nineteenth-century inn. Both parts have dark wood antique settles, and the bar has been assembled from an old sea chest.

With the sea being an often unwelcome neighbour, the inevitable stories have arisen that the New Inn was a haven for smugglers and pirates, who would divide up their ill-gotten gains in the darkened rooms. And the cool, north-facing kitchen wing was also used as a temporary mortuary when the bodies of unfortunate sailors were swept ashore. A walk along the broad sands towards Pendine brings the visitor to further victims of the sea. Here and there the bones of wrecked ships poke up through the sand, and muddy roots mark the site of forests drowned over 7,000 years ago.

The seaside village of Amroth lies about 3 miles north-east of Saundersfoot, reached off the A477 along a minor road from Stepaside or Wiseman's Bridge. The inn is situated at the east end, beside the coast road to Pendine. Bar snacks and meals, self-catering accommodation. Open 11 a.m.–3 p.m., 5.30–11 p.m.

CENARTH

(SN 269 414)

Hundreds of visitors pause at Cenarth every year to visit the fishing museum, or walk along the rocky riverbank to view the falls (actually a series of cascades) and the photogenic seventeenth-century corn-mill. There were beavers here in the Middle Ages, but now only salmon hurling themselves up the rapids can be seen in the Teifi.

When in season this delectable fish features on the menu at the White Hart, a long, whitewashed building at the head of the bridge. The sign says sixteenth century, but the architecture proclaims an eighteenth-century date for the pub. There is a restaurant housed in a refurbished bakehouse, which was built up against the side of the older house, and is reached along a passageway beside the back-to-back fireplaces. Both inglenooks are so large that you can sit and eat your meal beneath the great curving lintels.

In the bar itself all is dark, glowing wood, some original, some brought from a nearby derelict mansion. Mounted pheasants take wing from the beam over the hearth, and on the walls are framed prints recalling the strong fishing tradition of the village. There is even a coracle outside, a wicker-framed tar boat, which for centuries has been the only craft used by the Teifi fishermen.

Of a similar age and plan to the White Hart is the nearby Three Horseshoes, and a fishing theme dominates the decor here too. Outside in the yard is a splendid little thatched cottage, which has recently been refurbished and

Cenarth, the White Hart

opened as a separate bar. This is believed to be the original alehouse of the village referred to in a document of 1760, although the date 1805 is carved into the beam over the fireplace. Once through the low door customers find themselves in a single long room dominated by a huge inglenook and a spacious roof lined with blackened logs and gorse underthatch. Here and there stuffed owls and pheasants perch on the twisted beams. While a local historian has proclaimed this building to be medieval, it may be no older than the inscribed date, yet it epitomizes the plain and humble dwellings many countryfolk would have lived in centuries ago.

Cenarth village lies on the A484 Cardigan to Carmarthen road, about 3 miles west of Newcastle Emlyn. Bar snacks and meals. Open 12–3 p.m., 6.30–11 p.m.

The Pendre Inn, CILGERRAN
(SN 196 429)

Despite the many alterations and refurbishments carried out over the years at the Pendre Inn, customers can hardly fail to recognize the oldest part of this ancient hostelry. The massively thick slate-stone walls (some leaning out of vertical), blackened rough-hewn beams, and a great *simne fawr* (the local name for an inglenook) all indicate an early origin. The creaking sign outside proclaims a fourteenth-century date, and while this is a rather optimistic estimate there is little doubt that the Pendre is one of the oldest surviving pubs in west Wales.

The main bar and adjoining pool room are pleasant enough, but the real treasure of this village pub is the lounge, which was formerly the hall of the original house. The aforementioned early features are all confined to this room, which is remarkably small considering the size of the fireplace and thickness of the walls. On the front side there is a two-storeyed bay with tiny windows, and it is said that flagons of beer used to be passed through these unglazed openings to the men who looked after travellers' horses outside. This bay closely resembles those at the seventeenth-century Laleston Inn and Old Swan Inn, Glamorgan (see pp. 41–2, 52–6) and may indicate the age of the Pendre. But behind the imposing bay window are clear signs of an older and much humbler dwelling, with smaller windows and a lower roofline. The thick walls may be all that remains of a late medieval hall, once open to the rafters

Cilgerran, the Pendre: a conjectural reconstruction of the inn in its earliest form. The main fireplace appears to have had a wattle and daub hood, and may have replaced an open hearth. In the seventeenth century an upper floor was inserted into the hall and a storeyed bay window added to the front

and heated by a small hearth on the floor. An examination of the outside walls shows that the building has been heightened and the upper floor inserted. Certainly the rear stair wing is an addition, and so too is the bay window. Although there is a large fireplace on the ground floor there is no sign of a flue above, and it may be that the fireplace had a wattle and daub hood, an unusual feature found mainly in this area of west Wales.

A far better-known relic of old Cilgerran is the castle, which was built around 1223 by the Norman Earl of Pembroke. The distinctive twin towers, dominating a wooded gorge on the Teifi, have long attracted the admiration of sightseer and historian. Artists such as Richard Wilson and Turner have captured Cilgerran Castle's romantic appeal on canvas. This stronghold was the impetus for the development of the town, and under its protective wing the little borough of Cilgerran grew. From medieval times onwards two fairs were held here annually, and nineteenth-century travellers record that as many as 20,000 cattle were offered for sale. The narrow streets were packed with buyers and sellers, and this was considered to be a 'small' fair! Alas, those early tourists were all enamoured with the castle, and have left us with no mention of the Pendre. It may have been one of the inns where the Revd J. Evans tried to find accommodation on a market day early in the nineteenth century; but it being packed out the worthy gentleman was forced to seek shelter elsewhere.

Like nearby Cenarth, the stretch of the river below the town was once renowned for its salmon fisheries, and the Elizabethan historian George Owen wrote that 'the cheifest weir of all Wales is to be seen here . . . built of strong timber frames and artificially wrought therein with stones'. As many as 140 salmon were caught in traps along the weir, 'the fish being most excellent, and for fatness and sweetness exceeding those of other rivers'. Now much rarer, the salmon still makes an appearance on the menu at pubs along the Teifi.

Cilgerran town and castle lie 2 miles south-east of Cardigan, reached from either the A484 Newcastle Emlyn road, or the A478 to Narberth. Bar snacks and meals. Open 11.30 a.m.–3.30 p.m., 6–11 p.m.

Serjeant's Inn, EGLWYSWRW
(SN 142 385)

'After a tedious and fatiguing stage across the mountains . . . to be met with a decent public house must be highly gratifying', wrote the Pembrokeshire antiquarian Richard Fenton, *c.* 1811. In the days before the advent of fast, comfortable vehicles and (relatively) smooth roads, such sentiments were heartfelt.

The Serjeant's Inn is a large whitewashed building vying with the parish church for pride of place in the small village. The symmetrical façade with long sash windows, bay windows and a pentice is a legacy of eighteenth- and nineteenth-century refurbishing, but the bar room itself is the original seventeenth-century part. There is the usual *simne fawr* with a blocked passage on one side which led into the adjoining 'courtroom'. One of the fireside benches has an inscription 'R. Richard 1795', and is said to be a memorial seat brought from the church.

The inn is reputed to be haunted by the ghost of a lady, but the landlord could unfortunately supply no more details! There were some strange goings-on here in the sixteenth century too, if we believe the tales told by local people to the historian George Owen (1552–1613). In the graveyard opposite the inn stood the medieval chapel of St Erw, but nobody dared bury their dead within the sacred precinct since any interment was found cast up out of the ground by the following morning. 'Therefore they hold opinion that their holy saint will not have any bedfellows with him', wrote Owen.

At one time the inn provided accommodation and rest not only for antiquarians, but also for the circuit judges travelling between the county towns of Haverfordwest and Cardigan. 'Here during the stay of the itinerant counsel, a tribunal is constituted for trying all offences against the dignity of the bar; in carrying on which mock process, an infinite deal of wit, humour and festivity is excited,' recorded Fenton. The infamous Judge Jeffreys is also said to have stayed here, and one of the upstairs bedrooms has a door with an oval hatch in it, through which messages were allegedly passed to the reclusive man. The creaking inn sign depicts a dour, periwigged face – perhaps the judge himself?

This association with travelling serjeants-at-law could have given rise to the pub's name, and the adjoining courtroom may have been a replacement for the medieval manor and court, which lay just outside the village. But equally the name could have had a military origin, since an armoury house stood nearby. 'This Armour House', wrote George Owen, 'for beauty, strength and good order . . . excelleth any other in Wales.' In it the local militia would keep their pikes, halberds and primitive firearms, until needed for practice in the surrounding fields.

The small village of Eglwyswrw lies between the Preseli Mountains and the sea, on the A487 Fishguard to Cardigan road. Bar snacks and meals, accommodation. Open 12–2 p.m., 5.30–11 p.m.

FISHGUARD
(SM 957 370)

With the sea figuring so strongly here it comes as no surprise to find pubs such as the Ship Inn, the Sailor's Rest, and the Ship and Anchor; but the local agricultural community is not forgotten, with the Farmer's Arms. None of the pubs here is very old, and this small stone eighteenth-century building is one of the more attractive, huddled beside its larger neighbour, the Town Hall. The interior has been modernized, although the original fireplace, which must have been impressive to judge by the size of the chimney, is still blocked up.

Across the road stands the mirror-image Royal Oak, which has a large beam-ceilinged restaurant extension at the rear. Over the front door is an inscription which records the peace treaty signed here between French and English forces following the last invasion of Britain, in 1797. The French fleet had in fact been aiming for Ireland, but decided instead to cause havoc on the mainland. Since most of the force was made up of convicts, discipline was almost non-existent, and the invasion degenerated into farce when the army discovered a cache of Portuguese wine salvaged by farmers from a wreck. With the arrival of the local militia the inebriated foreigners gave up the fight, having been greatly intimidated by the stout-hearted Fishguard women wielding pitchforks!

The town of Fishguard lies on the coast between Cardigan and St David's, and can be reached from either Haverfordwest or Cardigan via the A40. Bar snacks and meals, and restaurant, open 11 a.m.–3 p.m., 7–11 p.m.

Swanlake Inn, JAMESTON
(SS 055 989)

'Masons were so skillfull in ould tyme in these countries that most Castles and houses of any account were builded with vaultes verye stronglie and substanciallye wrought,' wrote George Owen, *c.* 1600. Those buildings admired by Owen nearly 400 years ago still moulder away in the woods and valleys of south Pembrokeshire, their survival due mainly to the strength and durability of their construction. Some are still lived in and have been outwardly modernized, but there is no disguising the rugged vaults and the ponderous chimney stacks which grace (if that is the word) the older houses. The so-called 'flemish' round chimneys really have nothing to do with the immigrants who settled in this area during the twelfth-century, and local craftsmen probably adopted the idea from the stone castles of the Norman invaders. In the villages of Lydstep, Lamphey, Penally and St Florence can be found the crumbling remains of these distinctive chimneys, having long outlived the houses they once warmed.

Jameston, the Swanlake Inn: a central-entry house with a typical Pembrokeshire chimney-stack

The massive square chimney at the Swanlake Inn is later in date than the more refined round types and, along with the rest of the building, probably dates from the late seventeenth, or eighteenth century. One can never be too sure with Pembrokeshire houses, though, for there is more than one example of a fairly modern cottage built up against a much older chimney! Inside, the lounge has a commodious inglenook with a modern railway sleeper for a lintel – the only relic of the time when the pub was called the Railway, after a now-defunct halt on the Tenby–Pembroke line. Birdwatchers will be disappointed to learn that there is no swan-filled lake here, and the present name recalls a bay on the rocky coast nearby. On one side of the hearth is a massive stone projection containing a clay bake-oven. Such ovens are a common feature in old houses where most of the cooking was done in the largest (and sometimes only) fireplace. The practice was to heat up the oven with red-hot coals from the fire, then scrape out the ashes and put in the food to be cooked. In one pub the cook could tell if the oven was at the right temperature if she could hold her bare arm inside for twenty seconds without flinching! The clay oven may have been imported from Devon, since examples are also known from Glamorgan. The whole building has been thoroughly restored in recent years, and the rear stable wing turned into a large games room. Anyone wishing to learn more about the domestic architecture of Pembrokeshire should certainly visit Tenby, where the beautifully restored Tudor Merchant's House gives a vivid taste of life in a sixteenth-century home.

Jameston is situated on the A4139 mid-way between Tenby and Pembroke. Bar meals. Open 12–3 p.m., 6–11 p.m. (Monday–Thursday), 12–11 p.m. (Friday and Saturday).

The Old Moathouse, KIDWELLY
(SN 408 070)

Dwarfed by the towering walls and battlements of Kidwelly Castle, the Old Moathouse is hardly the most obvious relic of this historic borough; but do not pass it by. Across the river the tall spire of the priory church catches the attention, though it is the hulking ruin of the thirteenth-century fortress which draws most visitors to Kidwelly. But the inn is one of the very few early domestic buildings which have survived to this day, and in a century when the town has lost so many older and charming buildings this is no mean feat. Old photographs and etchings alone recall the stone medieval houses which lined the streets, and even the replacing of thatched roofs with less combustible, but more boring, materials has brought about striking changes. In the early years of this century virtually every house in Water Street was thatched; now only the Mason's Arms retains its traditional hairpiece. The thick front wall of the pub is said to have been part of the fortified boundary wall of the old town; but this is most improbable, and the building may be no earlier than the eighteenth century.

The castle and borough of Kidwelly was founded in the early twelfth century by the ambitious and worldly Bishop Roger of Salisbury. He also established the priory on the opposite side of the river as a cell of Benedictine monks from Sherborne in Dorset. Piecemeal rebuilding in stone transformed the earth and timber fort into one of the strongest castles in south Wales, and in the late thirteenth century the townsfolk received a grant to enable them to build a wall around their town. The shattered walls can still be seen at the backs of houses and gardens, having long outlived any defensive purpose, but still defining the old centre. But the area enclosed was small and cramped, and by as early as the fourteenth century houses were being built in the vicinity of the priory, so that in time there were practically two towns here, old and new

Kidwelly, Old Moathouse Inn: Cutaway reconstruction of the inn, *c.* 1800

Kidwelly. When the Welsh, led by Owain Glyndwr, rose up in rebellion in the early fifteenth century, the old town stood in the forefront of the attack on the castle. The houses were razed and the gatehouse burnt. This attack signalled the decline of the old centre at the expense of the new; when the Tudor antiquarian John Leland visited Kidwelly around 1536 he wrote, 'the old Toun is near desolate', and a survey of 1609–13 noted that there were only eighteen properties within the walls, most of the land being used as gardens. In the early years of the nineteenth century, Samuel Lewis was busy compiling his *Topographical Dictionary of Wales*, and in the entry on Kidwelly he brusquely referred to the 'hovels' and 'thatched cottages of very inferior appearance'. At least this comparative neglect preserved it from the sweeping changes inflicted on the 'new' centre, so that the castle, town walls, and enclosed cottages preserve something of the atmosphere of a small Welsh medieval settlement.

One of the properties referred to in the seventeenth-century survey could well have been the Old Moathouse, though there is no record to prove it was an inn at that time. In fact, the actual date of the building is uncertain. The landlord unhesitatingly plumps for the sixteenth century, and certainly the rugged stone walls, massive chimney stack and rough-cut beams look hundreds of years old. But the plan, with two small rooms on either side of a cross-passage, is typical of many eighteenth- and nineteenth-century poor cottages in rural Carmarthenshire; and when the building was being renovated a zinc firemark dated 1740 was discovered in the blocked up inglenook. Some of the crooked ceiling beams are said to have come from a ship, but the slots and holes in the timbers simply indicate the former position of a removed lath and plaster partition. On the first floor the rough and uneven trusses no longer support a steep thatch roof, since fire regulations prevented the owner from carrying out an authentic restoration, and the inn was re-roofed at a higher level with slates. However, the most remarkable thing about the Moathouse is the amazing array of antiques and bric-a-brac which crowd the ground-floor rooms. Chests, clocks, crockery, dolls, dressers, glassware, guns, pots, pans and paintings fill every available nook and cranny in the place – this is more of an antique shop than a pub! At the side of the big fireplace a door leads to the spacious bar/lounge/dining room, which is entirely modern but rebuilt on early foundations uncovered during restoration work. The emphasis here is on good food and comfortable surroundings, and from the beer garden customers are treated to a fine view of the grim castle, at peace now after centuries of bloodshed and war.

The inn stands beside the castle gate in Kidwelly, 8 miles south of Carmarthen, or 9 miles north-west of Llanelli, along the A484. M4 junction 48. Bar snacks and meals, accommodation. Open all day.

The Ram Inn, LAMPETER
(SN 590 467)

One of the more delightful of the many cottage pubs in this area of rural West Wales, the Ram is a neat, whitewashed building guarded by an old oak, in an eyecatching position on the drovers road to Llandovery. It claims to be sixteenth century, but all the architectural details point to a date around 1800. Despite the rustic exterior the inside is surprisingly modern and roomy, with a plush leather-padded bar, a beamed ceiling and whitened walls. There would originally have been two small rooms separated by the entrance passage and stairwell, but all partitions have been swept away to create a spacious yet homely atmosphere. There is a real fireplace in the lounge, although the brick hearth is a poor substitute for the cavernous inglenook which must lie hidden behind. A very low door leads to the rear lounge, where a further modernized wing houses a restaurant. From the wall over the dartboard a ram's head gazes sheepishly down at the customers; there are even ram's head designs on the metal fireguard.

George Borrow would have passed the Ram on his way from Lampeter to Llandovery in 1854: 'After walking very briskly for an hour I came to a very small hamlet consisting of not more than six or seven houses, of these three seemed to be public houses.' Standing by the roadside were three men who turned out to be the landlords of the pubs, who politely offered to buy the traveller a drink in their own premises. But Borrow soon realized that he was expected to return the compliment. 'Then it would come to this,' said Borrow. 'I should receive three pints from you three, and you three would receive nine from me.'

'I see your honour is a ready reckoner,' came the reply. But Borrow declined the deceptively generous offer, and hurried on his way.

The Ram stands in the village of Cwmann, 1 mile south-east of Lampeter, on the A482 to Llandovery. Other pubs in the area, similar in both age and architecture to the Ram, include the Talbot at Tregaron, and the Ship Inn at Pennant near Aberaeron. Bar meals and restaurant. Open 11 a.m.–11 p.m.

The White Hart, LLANDDAROG
(SN 503 166)

A sign on the green proudly announces to the passer-by the accolade of Best Kept Village awarded to Llanddarog in 1961 and 1973, and there seems to be no reason why this hilltop settlement should not win again in future years. The houses and cottages are huddled around the parish church, which crowns the summit of the hill, encircled by trees. Pride of place is reserved for the White Hart inn, arguably the most photogenic pub in west Wales. The bare stone

Llanddarog, the White Hart

walls, leaded windows and undulating thatched roof succeed in conveying an impression of great age, and there is a story that it was constructed in the fourteenth century to house the workers building the adjacent church. But in fact the plan of the inn is shared by many eighteenth-century houses in this area of Wales, and the characteristic thatching is only a rare survivor of a once common feature.

Elderly villagers still remember when the interior was partitioned off into small, low rooms, with a central passageway leading through to the stables at the back; but all internal walls have come down and there is now one long and spacious bar-lounge, with a heavy beamed ceiling and stone inglenooks at either end. More modern extensions at the rear have greatly increased the accommodation here, but by far the most impressive part of the inn is the adjoining dining room, which has been converted from the old stables and cartshed. Spare a glance too for the intricately carved dark oak settles, which look ancient but were made in the last century by a local craftsman. Although one might think that the White Hart offers the perfect surroundings for a ghost, there are no tales of any hauntings, and no spirits (other than the bottled variety) have been seen. Nevertheless there is a morbid association with the stone bench outside, since pallbearers on their way to the churchyard would rest the coffin on the slab while popping inside for a quick drink.

Llanddarog village lies just off the A48 dual carriageway between Cross Hands and Carmarthen. Bar meals and restaurant. Open 12–3 p.m., 6.30–11 p.m.

The King's Head, LLANDOVERY
(SN 767 343)

Llandovery in Welsh means the church by the waters, a reference to the many streams and rivers which flow down from the Carmarthenshire uplands to merge here with the meandering Tywi. These watery obstacles helped defend the small town established in the shadow of a twelfth-century Norman castle, but it was not until the late thirteenth century, after King Edward I had defeated the Welsh princes, that the countryside was quiet enough for stable economic growth. Even so, the rivers and castle walls failed to hold back the army of Owain Glyndwr, and the ravaged town was slow to recover. Richard III no doubt cheered up the townsfolk by granting them a charter of privileges, including a monopoly of pubs in the district: 'There shall be no tavern in this land . . . except in the borough of Llandovery' runs the clause. It may be due to this that the town has boasted of so many pubs and inns. Even so, when John Leland passed this way around 1536 he saw only 'one strete, and that poorely builded of thatchid houses'. One of these buildings was probably the King's Head, which stands opposite the town hall on what was the eastern edge of the medieval borough.

Apart from the castle ruins, the King's Head is probably the oldest surviving building in town, and although its age is uncertain the plan is typical of late medieval houses, with a hall, cross-passage and lateral fireplace. Generation after generation of occupiers have left their mark on the building; altering and modifying, concealing and destroying. The present owners have extensively refurbished the inn over the last twenty years, uncovering many lost features including the main inglenook fireplace, and a section of oak panelling which had been hidden behind a flimsy partition wall. This has been carefully restored to its former glory and is now set up in the residents' lounge on the first floor.

The fireplace and thick stone walls are all that remains of the early building, although the entrance passage which survived until recently could well have marked the original entry way. The upper parts of the walls have been rebuilt and the first floor and attic put in. By tradition this work was carried out in the reign of Charles I, whose head adorns the inn sign. Certainly the panelling and sagging beams belong to the first half of the seventeenth century.

In the following century a small house was built at the back of the inn, with an archway leading to a rear yard where travellers' horses were stabled overnight. This house has now been incorporated into the bar, and it was here in 1799 that a local drover, David Jones, founded the Bank of the Black Ox. As a teenager Jones worked at the pub, and evidently gained the trust of his fellow drovers and cattle dealers – who would place their money in his keeping while they were on the long road to the English markets. From these simple beginnings Jones ended up as a wealthy man and high sheriff of Carmarthenshire. His grandsons carried on the business and opened branches at Llandeilo and Lampeter. Then around 1909 the bank was incorporated into Lloyds and the black ox was changed for a black horse. Several nineteenth-century banking documents were discovered recently and are now displayed on the bar walls.

Another series of prints in the lounge provides an illustrated history of the exploits of a more famous local man, Thomas Jones (c. 1530–1609), better known as Twm Sion Catti. His career paralleled that of David Jones, although reputedly his money was gained in more dubious ways and his adventures have become part of Welsh folklore. In reality Twm was a man of letters, well versed in heraldry, and with bardic aspirations, who ended his days as the happily married squire of Ystradffin. In his fictional role as trickster and highwayman, Twm frequently visited the Llandovery pubs when not on the run from the inefficient sixteenth-century police force. His cave-hideout at Ystradffin continues to be visited by hundreds of tourists – even if Twm may never have gone there himself!

Vicar Rhys Pritchard (c. 1573–1644) was a contemporary of Twm who also frequented the town pubs for a drink or two – or three. Pritchard used to plead with drovers to 'be honest in dealings . . . and to refrain from imbibing too freely'. But in his younger days Pritchard used to spend more time imbibing than preaching, and was often carried home in a wheelbarrow. 'Bad as we may be, we are not half so bad as the parson', bemoaned the hardest drinkers. But divine guidance to the straight and narrow came in a most surprising way. One day the inebriated vicar amused himself and his cronies by giving beer to a goat to drink. The animal fell into a drunken stupor and was followed shortly after by its tormentor. The following day Pritchard tried the same trick again, but the goat knew well enough to turn away from the proffered pint. 'My God! is this poor dumb creature wiser than I?' exclaimed Pritchard, and walked out of the pub for good.

His later life was in complete contrast, and his collection of religious homilies *Cannwyll y Cymry* was as popular in seventeenth-century Wales as *The Pilgrim's Progress* was in England. His imposing mansion in High Street, Neuadd Newydd, was demolished earlier this century, a sad loss for the town. Now only the pubs remain, an irony the younger vicar may have appreciated.

Llandovery lies in the Vale of Tywi on the A40 between Brecon and Llandeilo. Bar snacks and meals, accommodation. Open 11.30 a.m.–3. p.m., 5.30–11 p.m.

Priory Inn, MILFORD HAVEN
(SM 903 073)

Although the Priory Inn has been a public house for only a few years, it is nevertheless one of the oldest buildings included in this book, since it formed part of the thirteenth-century priory of St Mary.

In the reign of Henry I a colony of pious and hard-working monks from the Breton Abbey of Tiron arrived in Britain and established religious centres in Scotland, Hampshire and at St Dogmael's near Cardigan in west Wales. The austere and simple lifestyle of these settlers inspired some pious feelings in the ruthless Normans, and they were presented with gifts of land and the revenues of local churches. Around 1200 Adam de Rupe, lord of Roche castle near Haverfordwest, granted land bordering the great inland waterway of Milford Haven to the monks of St Dogmael's, and in a wooded valley by the shore they established a priory cell. For the next four centuries a small group of devout men lived, worshipped and died here, rarely venturing beyond the cloistered walls. To them the world was the priory church and its surrounding buildings, the dormitories, kitchens, dining hall, stores and guest lodgings.

All of the monastic property was seized by the Crown at the Reformation in 1536. The last prior of Pill wisely relinquished control of the House, and was granted a pension of £10. Wealthy secular landowners then eagerly bought the estates and buildings, filling the royal coffers with much needed money.

Thus the priory church suffered the same fate as many others; the Catholic images were removed and destroyed, the building stripped of valuable materials, and the remaining shell was left to decay. Some of the adjoining buildings, however, could be better adapted to secular use, and part of the south cloister range was later converted into a farmhouse. It is not unlikely

Milford Haven, the Priory Inn: a view of the restored vaulted cellar of the medieval priory, now part of the inn

that parts of the priory had already been turned over to more private use. Towards the end of the Middle Ages the monastic ideal had become sadly tarnished, Houses were understaffed, and the abbots and priors indulged in lifestyles little different from wealthy secular landowners. Look at the sumptuous abbots' houses at Neath, Llanthony, Much Wenlock and Castle Acre, for instance. Though on a much smaller scale, the Priory Inn appears to incorporate the gable end of such a dwelling, for on the first floor there is a Tudor doorway, which indicates that this part of the building at least is not as old as the rest of the thirteenth-century priory.

Looking at the building today, the inn appears to be a shapeless mass of rough stone, with irregular gables, stumpy chimneys and a few small windows scattered here and there. The heart of the inn is the remaining fragment of a medieval building – apparently the end wing of the cloister range. Wrapped around this on three sides is the post-Reformation farmhouse and a little cottage, with its end wall bending inwards at an odd angle to make way for an earlier mill leat which runs alongside. The farmhouse with its beamed ceiling and large inglenook forms the bar, and the delightfully restored cottage is now the lounge; but the most outstanding part of the inn is the central lounge, which is housed in the vaulted undercroft of the medieval range. Large windows and an open log fireplace have been cut into the thick stone walls, but originally this would have been a dark and cheerless storeroom, and the main living area would have been on the first floor. This room is now reached by an outside stone stair, but is not original since it blocks two windows visible from inside the bar.

About four years ago the Priory Inn was opened as a public house, and before then it was carefully restored from a state of almost total dereliction. Pre-restoration photographs on the lounge walls show what a great task this was. The old farmhouse can also be glimpsed in some of the prints and etchings which decorate the walls, though in some it is a large sawmill which dominates the view. All trace of this industrial venture has been removed from the valley, apart from the mill-pond and leat.

Because of its fairly remote setting and scanty remains, the medieval priory did not attract more than local interest among past antiquarians, although Richard Fenton, the Pembrokeshire historian, was captivated by the rural charm of the valley with its 'cottages among the ruins'. 'If monks were capable of happiness' he wrote in *c.* 1811, 'surely those of Pill might have felt themselves so.' The farmers of the valley may not have had such a rosy image of monastic life, since they frequently dug up the mortal remains of monks in their gardens! Today only one of the arches of the central tower remains above ground, and the rest of this ancient religious house is hidden, awaiting rediscovery by future archaeologists.

Pill Priory lies just under a mile north-west of Milford Haven town centre. If approaching from Haverfordwest via the A4076, then turn right at Steynton crossroads, and follow the road for 1 mile to where a signposted right turn leads under a railway bridge to the priory. Bar snacks and meals. Open 11 a.m.–11 p.m.

The White Hart, ST DOGMAELS, CARDIGAN

(SN 164 460)

Until the Dissolution of the Monasteries brought to an end the supremacy of the Catholic Church in England and Wales, the Abbey of St Dogmael's was the cultural and spiritual heart of this little Teifi-side village. Yet despite the holy aspirations of the inhabitants, it would appear that the monks were the most regular customers of the local pub! In 1402 the bishop of St David's Cathedral complained to the abbot that the monks were frequently to be found in the tavern drinking, gossiping and, horror of horrors, fraternizing with the opposite sex. Even by the standards of the later Middle Ages, when the harsh monastic disciplines had been relaxed, this sort of behaviour could not be ignored, and the bishop ordered that no women should be lodged in the village. One monk was ordered to give his yearly allowance of wine to the poor as a penance. To further prevent the brothers straying from the straight and narrow, the 'vice' of gathering around a cheery fire for a chat was to be allowed only on frosty days.

This sort of behaviour was just the excuse the king's commissioners needed to recommend closing the monasteries in 1536, and with the passing of years and the stone robbing antics of the locals, the splendour of St Dogmael's was reduced to grey ruin. The monk's tavern has gone too, its place taken by others built in more recent times. Of these the White Hart is the oldest, possibly of eighteenth-century date, though the interior has been restored over the years. It is set into the hillside so that the two bar-lounges are on different levels, the lower with a worn flagstone floor, beamed ceiling and a modern brick fireplace sprinkled with horsebrasses. A framed newspaper cutting on the wall chronicles the story of the tippling monks.

The village of St Dogmaels lies just under a mile west of Cardigan town centre, on the B4546 to Poppit Sands. Bar meals. Open 11 a.m.–3 p.m, 6–11 p.m.

The Old Cross Keys, SWANSEA
(SS 657 929)

Apart from the castle, the only other early building in Swansea to have survived Victorian modernization and a devastating raid in the last war is the Cross Keys. Now looking very forlorn among its more modern neighbours, the building has recently been extended and refurbished on a lavish scale, so much so that the mock-medieval accretions are in danger of overshadowing the original inn. This could justly be claimed the oldest public house in Wales, since it was built around 1330 by Henry de Gower, Bishop of St David's (1328–47), though in fact it only became an inn at the end of the seventeenth century. But what is the connection between a medieval prelate and a public house?

Swansea, Cross Keys Inn: the seventeenth-century façade in St Mary's Street

Swansea, Cross Keys Inn: a surviving fourteenth-century window

Bishop Henry, born on the nearby peninsula from which his name derives, founded an almshouse or 'hospital' within the walled city of Swansea, dedicated to the patron St David. The foundation charter of 1332 mentions that it was established 'for the support of other poor chaplains and laymen deprived of bodily health. . . . Lest priests, blind, decrepit, or infirm and other poor men, in the bishopric of St David's, be at any time destitute of food, and begging, to the scandal of the clergy and of the Church . . .'. This worthy institution survived until the Reformation when it was sold by the Crown, and passed into the hands of Sir George Herbert (see Baron's Court, p. 61). During the sixteenth and seventeenth centuries the various buildings which formed the hospital were put to other uses, and one of them was adapted as a shop, then later as an inn. With the passing of time all the other medieval buildings were demolished and the location of the hospital forgotten.

One day in 1844 Colonel George Francis, a founder-member of the Royal

Institution of South Wales, was riding his horse through the narrow Victorian alleyways, and entered a yard at the rear of a neighbouring pub: 'I observed in a gable of some old premises, the outlines of arches which struck me as similar in character to those in Swansea castle.' The arches he saw were the original fourteenth-century windows in the rear wing of the pub, and which today can be clearly seen from the roadside. The original function of this building is unknown, but the presence of a fireplace on the upper floor and an open roof with carved trusses indicates that it was a first-floor hall, perhaps the residence of the chaplain or attendant priests. Photographs on the lounge wall show how dilapidated the Cross Keys had become by the early years of this century. During the 1950s vital repairs were carried out on the building and the exterior rendering was stripped away to reveal some hidden features. The impressive storeyed bays on the St Mary Street side had to be rebuilt, and the decayed timberwork was carefully restored. Both bays were added to the medieval building in the seventeenth century, and originally contained two narrow shops separated by a passage leading to the rear wing. Marks of these alterations can be detected on the massive ceiling beams inside. Some reused fragments of a medieval roof truss stand guard on either side of a small seating area in the lounge, while other finds discovered here (including a stone cannonball and a silver shilling of Edward VI) can be seen in the nearby museum of the Royal Institution.

The Cross Keys stands opposite St Mary's church in the city centre. M4 junctions 44, 45. Bar snacks and meals. Open 11 a.m.–11 p.m.

Additional inns and taverns

Cardigan, The Eagle (SN 177 457)
Carmarthen, Angel Vaults (SN 413 200)
Haverfordwest, Carmarthen Arms (SM 957 157)
Llanwrda, Hafod Bridge Inn (SN 696–360)
Newcastle Emlyn, Bunch of Grapes (SN 308 407)
Newport, Golden Lion (SN 058 392)
Pennant, Ship Inn (SN 514 631)
Pont-ar-gothi, Cothi Bridge (SN 506 218)

2. SOUTH-EAST WALES

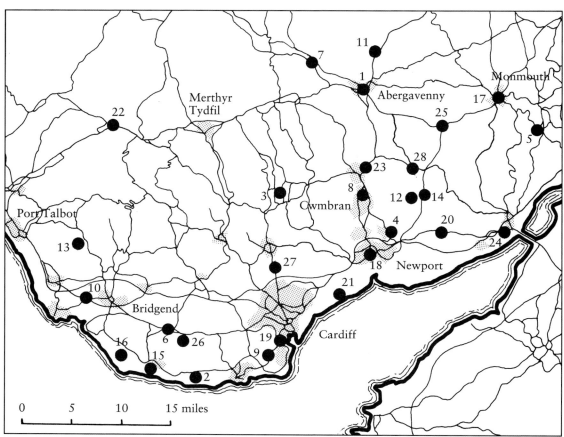

Merthyr Tydfil

Port Talbot

Bridgend

Cardiff

Newport

Abergavenny

Monmouth

Cwmbran

11
7
1
22
25
17
5
23
28
3
8
12 14
4
20
13
18
24
27
21
10
16 6 26
19
15 9
2

0   5   10   15 miles

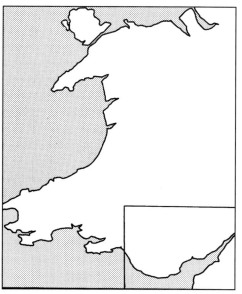

1. Abergavenny
2. Aberthaw
3. Blackwood
4. Caerleon
5. Clearwell
6. Cowbridge
7. Crickhowell
8. Cwmbran
9. Dinas Powis
10. Laleston
11. Llanfihangel Crucorney
12. Llangybi
13. Llangynwyd
14. Llantrisant

15. Llantwit Major
16. Monknash
17. Monmouth
18. Newport
19. Penarth
20. Penhow
21. Peterstone Wentloog
22. Pont Nedd Fechan
23. Pontypool
24. Pwllmeyric
25. Raglan
26. St Hilary
27. Thornhill
28. Usk

The King's Arms, ABERGAVENNY

(SO 300 141)

Abergavenny prides itself on being called the 'gateway to Wales', and, although it is a good six miles from the border, it is the first major town travellers encounter upon entering the country from Hereford. Like the neighbouring towns of Usk and Monmouth, Abergavenny owes its origins to the Romans, but the earliest surviving buildings date from the Middle Ages. The ruined castle and priory church are obvious monuments to the ambitious Normans but, alas, the humbler domestic buildings have suffered neglect and indifference for too long. During the 1950s and '60s some of the narrow, twisting medieval streets were swept away and replaced with wider thoroughfares and car-parks, and while this made parts of the town less cramped, many old timber-framed buildings were also destroyed. The most useful source of information concerning the lost houses of Abergavenny is a collection of sketches and articles by the Gwent local historian, Fred Hando (1888–1970), whose work featured regularly in the pages of the *South Wales Argus*. Hando was left to pick over the bones of the ruined buildings in Tudor Street, and in one crumbling basement saw the prison cell of the old west gatehouse. At Gunter's House in Cross Street, he saw a religious wall painting which had been taken from a hidden chamber in the attic, where persecuted Catholics once gathered in secret to celebrate Mass. This house fortunately still survives, and is marked with a plaque.

Beside the vanished west gate stands the King's Arms, now in impressive isolation since the demolition of the clustered streets and alleyways. It is a long, low whitewashed building with bowed walls, black painted sash windows (which seem to have wandered over the façade) and a cluster of striking red and yellow brick chimneys. Most attractive of all is the colourful coat of arms set up on the outside wall, said to be in commemoration of a visit by Charles II. Inside there are several rooms opening off a cross-passage – perhaps a relic of a medieval house? There are half-dismantled timber partitions and some finely carved ceiling beams, which indicate that this was a dwelling of some standing. Some of the details suggest an early seventeenth-century date, but it is clear that the building has been altered and added to over the years. The main bar has an amazingly bowed ceiling, and any tall customer walking down the middle will have to duck. This room is the headquarters of the local Royal Navy Association, which explains the flotilla of framed ships on the wall. In the last century the King's Arms had its own brewery run by Thomas Delafield, and one eminent Edwardian analyst considered the drink to be 'a wholesome and tonic beverage'; but more familiar brews are on tap today.

The town of Abergavenny lies in the Vale of Usk, at the junction of the A465 Hereford road, and the A40 Brecon to Monmouth road. Bar snacks and meals. Open 11 a.m.–3 p.m., 6–11 p.m.

The Blue Anchor, ABERTHAW
(ST 036 666)

It is hard now to believe that the muddy, meandering estuary of the little river Thaw was once a flourishing port dating, perhaps, back to Roman times. During the sixteenth and seventeenth centuries large amounts of brandy, tobacco and other luxuries were imported here, and so much money was made that the owners of quayside Marsh House decided to fortify their warehouse to prevent anyone making off with their impounded stock. Reckoned to be the last 'castle' built in Wales, Marsh House was sadly demolished a few years ago.

On the shore, and now lost to the wind and waves, stood the Limpert Inn and the Ship Inn. The former survived to be photographed earlier this century, and it is shown as a long, whitewashed thatched cottage, probably of seventeenth-century date. Here passengers would be forced to spend an uncomfortable night or two on cramped, makeshift beds, while waiting for a favourable wind to embark for the West Country.

Piracy was rife in these parts, and the local gentry were the worst of the lot, dealing and double-dealing with the freebooters, with little fear of any retribution from the law. The vicar of one Vale village complained of his flock that 'first they were pirates, next they were smugglers, then they became wreckers, and by this time there is not an honest man left among them'. Hardly surprising that the Blue Anchor Inn should be known as a smugglers' haunt, with its warren of small, low rooms, and stories of secret passages leading to nearby safe houses. Did pirates really leave their skiffs on the riverbank, and creep along dark and dripping tunnels burdened with contraband, to emerge from some hidey-hole in the thick walls of the inn? Hardly likely. In fact, the London Customs Board learned in 1734 how smuggled goods were brought ashore without the aid of tunnels. A local

Aberthaw, the Blue Anchor

official told how the pirates 'have always a Spye on the officer; and when they find him on one side of the river at Aberthaw, they'll land what they have on the other'. By the time the officer crossed the nearest bridge (some distance upstream) the gang had vanished with their booty: 'there is instances that they'd run goods in the daytime before the officers face in this Manner'!

The Blue Anchor is a chunk of limestone masonry topped with a thick, unruly mop of thatch. There is a large car-park across the road, and the flower-bedecked courtyard is a pleasant place to sit in the summer, when the leafy trees hide all sight of the Aberthaw power station and cement works. The Inn stands some distance away from the old port, and while it may have catered to the needs of seaborne travellers and the odd pirate, it was originally a farmhouse. Marsh Cottage across the road is just as old, but since the exterior has been modernized its age is not as obvious.

The inn has been authoritatively dated to the mid-sixteenth century, a quite respectable age for any Welsh house, and the traditional fourteenth-century date is, unfortunately, quite unfounded. It is possible, though by no means certain, that the lower bar (once the hall) is the oldest part of the house, and that the upper bar (formerly the kitchen) was added at a later date. The chamfer stops on the ceiling beams are different in each part, but this may be simply a case of saving the finer details for the better room. A lovely arched doorway wreathed in ivy leads into the old kitchen, with its great fireplace in the end wall. There is plenty of dark timber and lots of woodworm. One sagging beam is propped up by a tree trunk. A modern door leads to the lower bar and lounge, but look closely and you will see part of the original sixteenth-century arched door embedded in the later stonework.

Both the kitchen and hall have their own stairs built into the thick walls. How many generations of feet have worn down the oak treads? Beyond the kitchen a low, narrow and twisting passage leads into an eighteenth-century bakehouse, now a pleasant lounge with a large timber settle beside the great brick bake-oven. Note the ammonite fossil in the back wall of the fireplace. More beams and aged wood complement the bare stonework, and there is yet another lounge leading off. With so many rooms, nooks and stairways here, is it any wonder that tales of secret passages have grown around this old house?

The village of East Aberthaw lies just off the B4265 Llantwit Major road, about 4 miles west of Barry. Bar snacks and meals. Open 11 a.m.–11 p.m.

The Penllwyn Arms, BLACKWOOD
(ST 174 956)

Historic old pubs in the uplands of Glamorgan and Gwent are few and far between, but as if to make up for this scarcity the former mining town of Blackwood in Gwent can boast of the largest and most impressive public house in the county. Sixteenth-century Penllwyn lies hidden away on a hillside housing estate, virtually ignored by every pub guide and history book, and yet it is a building which epitomizes the confidence and social aspirations of the late Tudor gentry in Wales.

Penllwyn was built by a branch of the Morgan family of Machen, themselves offshoots of the Tredegar clan at Newport. Tredegar House is now justly recognized as one of the finest stately homes in Wales, but how many know of Penllwyn? The family was established around the middle of the sixteenth century by Edmund Morgan, an adept social climber whose three wives were drawn from the wealthiest and most influential local families. His descendants were sheriffs and MPs, though there is no truth to the story that one of his offspring was the notorious pirate, Henry Morgan. The last male heir was also named Henry, and was known as 'king of the hills'; 'His name is still mentioned with endearment by those who experienced his hospitality and benevolence' wrote Archdeacon Coxe in 1799. On Henry's death in 1725 the property was conveyed to his sister Florence, wife of Squire Jones of Llanarth. There were further upheavals in the nineteenth century when John Jones married the daughter of Sir Benjamin Hall (after whom Big Ben clock tower was named), thus merging Penllwyn with the rich Llanover estates.

Over the succeeding generations Penllwyn was used as a schoolhouse, nursery, nunnery, hotel and, after a period of neglect, as a public house. There have been inevitable changes over the years, as each occupier adapted the house to his own needs, but the exterior is little altered from the days when the squires of Penllwyn held sway over the poor farmers and yeomen of the Gwent valleys. The surrounding housing estate may not add to the grandeur of the setting, but the house itself stands alone, ringed by dry-stone walls and shaded by sycamore trees. When Archdeacon Coxe visited the Sirhowy valley there were a good deal fewer houses around: 'the ancient mansion is delightfully situated on the brow of the eminence overhanging the Sorwy, in the midst of arable and pasture grounds, which descend to the banks of the Rumney'.

The impressive façade of Penllwyn obscures the fact that there are two houses here, the original mid-sixteenth-century house of Edmund Morgan, and the more imposing edifice built around 1600 by his son, or grandson. The older house stands at the lower end of the building, now the public bar, and can be distinguished by the narrower windows and lower floor levels. We do not know the reason why this perfectly adequate house should have been vastly enlarged by the addition of another; it may simply have been a case of Tudor one-upmanship, an arrogant desire by the lord of the manor to impress upon all and sundry his wealth and social standing. Certainly it could hardly have failed to do so, with its stately porch, huge hall and rows of mullioned windows crowned with dormers. Formal symmetry was only reserved for the front, and the back of the house displayed an amazing array of turrets, chimneys, wings and lean-tos, that have now largely been modernized or swept away. Fortunately the landlord possesses an original ink sketch by Fred Hando which records these features.

Modern works have also disguised many internal features. The great fireplace of the hall can just be glimpsed behind rows of bottles, and the heavy ceiling beams are hidden beneath ornamental plaster. On the first floor there is a spacious dining area and function room, which is reached up a dog-leg stair so large it is housed in a projecting turret. From the top landing a rickety flight of stairs climbs to the attic, where huge oak trusses support the stone slated

Blackwood, Penllwyn Arms: a bird's-eye view of this minor gentry house *c.* 1600. The porch, great hall and rear wings were all added to a smaller and older house at the top right

roof. Servants would have slept here, while the more well-to-do occupants resided in greater comfort on the floor below.

In a house as old as Penllwyn it may come as no surprise to learn that there have been several reported hauntings and ghostly manifestations over the years. Mrs Mathews, a long deceased tenant, now walks the corridors late at night, keeping company with Henry Morgan, while on occasion closed doors open, lights flick on by themselves, and the scent of burning candles wafts through the house.

Blackwood lies in the Sirhowy valley, on the A4048 Newport to Tredegar road. From M4 junction 28 follow the dual carriageway signposted to Risca and Ebbw Vale, for about 5 miles, where a signposted turn at a roundabout

*leads to Tredegar and Blackwood. After another five miles the road enters
Pontllanfraith village, then pass through two roundabouts in the direction of
Ystrad Mynach. About 100 yards beyond the second roundabout, a right hand
turn leads up the hillside into a housing estate, and when another roundabout
is reached, take the last turning off, and Penllwyn can be seen beyond some
trees. Bar snacks and meals. Open 12–3 p.m., 6.30–11 p.m.*

CAERLEON
(ST 340 906)

The Romans had their *tavernae* here eighteen centuries ago, when Caerleon
was the great legionary fortress of *Isca*. They have long gone, and their
engineering and architectural ventures lie in ruins beneath modern roads and
houses. But in places archaeologists have rescued the past for posterity, and
sections of the Roman fort have been excavated and displayed to the public.
Antiquarians have long known of the amphitheatre on the edge of town,
although for centuries this great bowl-shaped earthwork was thought to have
been King Arthur's round table.

Beside the site of the old market hall stands the Old Bull Inn, one of the finest
early domestic buildings surviving in Caerleon – dating from the sixteenth and
seventeenth century. The interior is a wealth of bare stonework and aged timber,
with several rooms and seating areas leading off from the enlarged early core of
the building. The architectural history of the Bull is locked up in its stout walls;
and changes in the masonry, different carvings on beams and the shape of the
doors and windows all help to reconstruct the changing face of this house over
the centuries. The Old Bull was originally a town house belonging to a branch of
the Morgan family (see p. 26). The name of the pub is thought to recall the bull's
head crest of their Welsh ancestor, Bledri, though a less likely story claims it to
be a punning reference to Henry VIII's wife, Anne Boleyn!

The main bar now occupies the oldest part of the house, the great hall of
early sixteenth-century date. It is possible that the heavy oak-beamed ceiling is
not an original feature, and that the hall was once open to the roof. Anyone
entering the house around four hundred years ago would have passed through
an arched doorway into the lofty hall, with its carved roof trusses arching
overhead. Most of the general day-to-day activities took place in the hall itself,
and there would only have been additional small rooms on the other side of

Caerleon, Old Bull: a cutaway view *c.* 1600, showing the newly added rear wing and earlier hall block in front. Note the post-and-panel partition in the hall, since removed

the cross-passage, used for storage, probably with sleeping chambers over. The existing upper floor may have been added later in the sixteenth century to increase the accommodation. Many other changes to the fabric of the hall are almost imperceptible, but customers should have little trouble in recognizing the more modern windows and fireplaces, with their red brick surrounds.

Around 1600 a self-contained wing was added to the rear of the hall, and this served as the kitchen. The upper floor was reached by a small winding stair concealed within the thick wall beside the chimney. The stair still has a tiny wooden window (without any glass, typical of the period), although the stone steps have been removed and a more convenient stair serves the first floor. The reconstruction drawing shows the inn as it would have appeared soon after the early seventeenth-century alterations. When Fred Hando visited the Old Bull in 1925, the genial landlord permitted him to crawl around the attic, where he found a shaft in the floor that may have been the flue of a primitive privy. I contented myself with an inspection of the first-floor rooms and saw, as Hando did, a carved stone or plaster head embedded in a partition wall, which is thought to be a fragment of reused Roman work. Down in the cellar there is a low arched recess extending a few feet towards the river, which is also thought to be Roman. Without excavation there is no solid evidence to confirm this, but the arch could have been part of the drainage system for the baths, which lay in the yard behind the pub. There is also a legend of a secret passage leading from the cellar to sixteenth-century Priory House across the road. There are more tangible relics of Roman Caerleon here, though, for in the walls of the bar-lounge can be seen shaped blocks of pale yellow sandstone which almost certainly were robbed from the crumbling ruins of *Isca*.

Caerleon today is a little town full of clustered buildings and narrow streets, with a huge suburb growing larger each year. The archaeological heritage of the old town has, so far, held back any major redevelopment within the Roman walls. Caerleon in the nineteenth century was a very different place. 'I stood in its lonely main street – an empty thoroughfare where grass grows, lined by poor houses of stone . . . a wretched little hamlet', wrote Wirt Sykes in 1881. He lavished praises on the hospitality of the Gold Croft Inn, 'a poor little stone house with low walls, and no sign of life anywhere about it'. Sykes was only one of a long list of travellers who visited Caerleon to see (and in some cases, to take) its antiquities. One of the earliest was the twelfth-century cleric, Gerald of Wales, who visited the town in 1188: 'You can still see many vestiges of its one-time splendour', wrote Gerald. 'There are immense palaces with gilded roofs, which once rivalled the magnificence of ancient Rome.' His near contemporary, Geoffrey of Monmouth, linked the Roman 'City of the Legions' to the legendary court of King Arthur. It is an association which has continued to this day. In September 1856 Alfred, Lord Tennyson, stayed at Caerleon and gained some inspiration for his Arthurian poems 'The Idylls of the King'. His resting place was the Hanbury Arms, a sprawling group of whitewashed buildings few travellers can miss as they approach the town's awkward one-way system. The oldest part is the tall three-storey block on the river front, a rather plain, frowning façade which gives only hints of its age. Look at the windows with their arched heads – the same as those in the Bull and just as old. In the large oriel Tennyson wrote 'The Usk murmurs by the window as I sit like King Arthur in Caerleon', and a plaque on the wall commemorates his visit here. Another author to visit the Hanbury on a more regular basis was Arthur Machen, a native of the town. His supernatural and mystic tales have gained Machen something of a cult following today.

The Hanbury's main bar is housed in the magistrates room, a name which recalls the time when the building was used as a courthouse. This is probably the oldest part of the building, and the elegant dressed stone fireplace and carved beams indicate it was the showpiece of the house.

In one of the upstairs rooms is kept a rare survivor of nineteenth-century culinary techniques – a dog wheel; and no doubt there are animal lovers who are quite pleased that such devices are no longer used. It was simply a wooden wheel suspended from the ceiling and linked by gears to a spit in front of the kitchen fire. The unlucky mutt was placed in the wheel and made to 'walk', so turning the joint before the flames. One nineteenth-century writer described the curs used for this job as 'sharp little fellows . . . credited with sufficient intelligence to understand when a heavy dinner was to be dressed, for then they would make off, and leave the kitchen maid to turn the spit in their stead'!

The Hanbury has another surprising feature to be singled out: the ruined and overgrown tower at one end of the building is all that remains of the outer bailey of the medieval castle. At one time the tower was thought to be Roman, and it was used as a 'lock-up' for unruly drunks. Caerleon Castle was founded by the Normans in the late eleventh century, though the masonry defences were added in the thirteenth century by the Earl of Pembroke. From the battlements soldiers could keep a watchful eye on anyone entering the town, since the original timber bridge across the Usk lay alongside the inn. The first stone bridge was not built until the early nineteenth century and has proved such a hazard to modern traffic that it may soon be bypassed. Travellers' tales and old drawings provide graphic evidence of the picturesque, but unstable, nature of the original bridge. There is the story of a traveller on horseback, journeying between Chepstow and Caerleon one dark and stormy night in the late eighteenth century. Tired, wet and half-asleep, he crossed over the rickety bridge to a warm and safe haven at the Hanbury. When he looked out of the window the following morning, he saw to his horror that part of the bridge had been swept away except for a solitary plank, over which he had been carried by his horse! The shock of this realization proved fatal.

Having safely arrived on the far side of the bridge, thankful travellers would have found themselves on the road to Chepstow, first passing through a little village called, appropriately enough, the Village, or Caerleon *Ultra Pontem*. At the top of the single street is the early sixteenth-century Bell Inn, a lovely jumble of bare stonework, varying rooflines, and a huge lateral chimney-stack. Coaches stopped here in the eighteenth and nineteenth centuries to unload tired and shaken passengers, to warm themselves in front of the great stone fireplace, while awaiting some refreshments. Now different vehicles wait outside, but little else has changed. One obvious and necessary alteration has been the introduction of electric lights; but above the arch of the fireplace are two carved stone brackets which once held the original light source of the building – candles.

Like the Old Bull, this was almost certainly an open hall, the present ceiling being inserted in the early seventeenth century. The end lounge has a roughly built hearth which contrasts with the fine carved fireplace in the hall, and is also likely to be a seventeenth-century modification. There is said to be a blocked winding stair in one of the walls which rose to the full height of the house, so enabling the servants to climb to their dingy attic bedrooms without having to pass through the main chambers on the first floor. The room above the hall was the private chamber of the moderately wealthy owner, and there is another arched fireplace here with a beautifully carved timber mantelpiece. Customers leaving the Bell Inn may notice the ruins of a large building adjoining the north end. This was once a malt-house, and an old etching on display in the pub shows it complete and roofed, almost dwarfing its far older companion.

Caerleon village lies about 1½ miles north-east of Newport centre, just off M4 junction 25. Old Bull: bar snacks and meals. Open 11 a.m.–11 p.m. Hanbury Arms: bar snacks and meals. Open 12–11 p.m. (closed Sunday afternoon).

CLEARWELL, FOREST OF DEAN
(SO 571 080)

The photogenic village of Clearwell makes an ideal centre for exploring the historic Wye valley and Forest of Dean – that area of land which seems neither English nor Welsh, but a country apart. For centuries the undulating woodlands have been exploited by man, the wildlife hunted by Norman knights, the hills broken open by Roman and medieval miners, and the trees cut down for charcoal and pit-props. Today the countryside is more gently exploited by tourists, and one of the most popular venues here is the ancient mine at Clearwell. The underground workings and natural caverns open to the public form only a small part of the labyrinth below the hills. It may have been with an aim to guard their important iron mines that the Normans built a castle here, and later established a village in the valley below. This was initially known as Wellington, and then later as Clearwell, both references to the cold, fresh spring which bubbles out of the hillside behind the Wyndham Arms.

The inn is named after the last of the wealthy families which resided here, in a line stretching back to the fourteenth century when the building is said to have been the manor house of Sir John Joyce. The Wyndham is the largest and most prestigious of the village pubs, and has benefited from an extensive programme of restoration work carried out since 1973. On the wall of the reception area are photographs showing the work in progress, and how the inn then appeared, with many features hidden behind paper and plaster. Now the oak beams are revealed and the large stone fireplaces opened out. The oldest

Clearwell, the Butcher's Arms: this reconstruction shows the probable original appearance of the hall (now the lounge) in the seventeenth century. The mouth of a bake-oven can be seen beside the fireplace

part of the building is believed to be the rear wing tucked under the hillside, now containing the kitchens and dining area. The modernized bar and lounge occupy a right-angled wing jutting into the street. It is possible that the walls were originally timber-framed, but they have been encased in stonework since *c.* 1600, which appears to be the age of the surviving stone mullioned windows.

This period witnessed a considerable amount of rebuilding in Clearwell, as the remaining architectural details show. A little way along the road to the mines is the Tudor Farmhouse, a charming listed thirteenth-century building with external features pointing to a seventeenth-century face-lift. Just beyond stands the Butcher's Arms, and while not claiming such an early origin, the main part of the building is at least 300 years old. There have been some later additions and modern renovations, but fortunately without losing any of the charm and character of a traditional village local.

The oldest part of the building is the roadside wing which contains the lounge and games room, though this of course was not their original function. One of the rooms must have been the hall, and the other a kitchen; but which was which? Both have large inglenooks with bake-ovens, so cooking could have been carried out in either room. The position of the original front door is uncertain too, since the existing entrance is a later alteration. Slots and holes in the two central ceiling beams show that the hall and kitchen were separated by a lost third room with half-timbered walls; so perhaps this contained the entrance lobby and stair.

Clearwell lies 2 miles south of Coleford, off the A4136 Monmouth to Mitcheldean road. The B4231 road from Lydney passes through the village. Bar snacks and meals, accommodation (at the Wyndham Arms). Open 11 a.m.–3 p.m., 5.30–11 p.m.

The Old Masons Arms, COWBRIDGE

(SS 993 746)

Among the numerous pubs and inns which boast a medieval date, the Old Masons Arms is one of the few genuinely early buildings. It was built up against the fourteenth-century defensive wall of the borough, which explains why the west gable wall is so thick. Cowbridge began life as a Roman settlement, but the present townscape owes much to the medieval borough founded here by the Normans around 1245. Probably as the result of a Welsh

Cowbridge, Old Masons Arms: a street scene in medieval Cowbridge. This shows the pub in the background, with the conjectured appearance of the demolished west gate on the right

uprising the townspeople began construction of a stone wall with four gateways to defend the central part of the town, but today only a short length of the wall and a single gate remain.

It is not known for how long the Old Masons Arms has been a pub, but it was ideally located next to the west gate (demolished in 1754) and would have been the first stopping place for weary and thirsty travellers entering the safety of the walled town. Alternatively its proximity to the gatehouse might suggest that it was the home of the porter responsible for collecting tolls and securing the gate each night. The pub has undergone only minimal alterations over the years; the main change came in the seventeenth century when the spacious, but cheerless, medieval hall was modernized with the addition of an upper floor, and the replacement of the open hearth with a stone fireplace. In the eighteenth century a small brewhouse was added at the back, and more recently an adjoining wing has been converted into a small dining room.

The interior is all dark stonework and even darker beams, and both bar-lounges are heated by the central fireplace. An arched stone door on the far side of the entrance passage clearly proclaims the antiquity of the inn, along with two narrow, pointed windows only visible from the street. They were blocked when the adjacent bay window was added in the seventeenth century. The Masons Arms has guest rooms on the first floor – but be warned! One room is said to be haunted, and a guest once spent the night sleeping downstairs in the lounge after seeing a pale lady flit through the wall.

The architectural heritage of Cowbridge has recently been examined by the Royal Commission on Ancient and Historical Monuments. Many shops and houses date from the sixteenth and seventeenth centuries, though often disguised behind Georgian and Victorian façades. The Bear Hotel is medieval, but does not look it; the elegant interior is the result of wholesale refurbishment in the eighteenth century. Some fragments of a beautifully carved stone fireplace indicate a medieval date. Further down the road stands the Duke of Wellington, another medieval survivor, though heavily restored and deprived of most early features on the ground floor. It is still a popular pub, with plenty of bare stonework and blackened beams.

Cowbridge is situated off the A48 about midway between Bridgend and Cardiff, M4 junction 35. The Old Masons Arms is at the west end of town, beside the market car-park. Bar snacks and meals, accommodation. Open 11.30 a.m.–3.30 p.m., 5.30–11 p.m.; Sunday: 12–4 p.m., 7–10.30 p.m.

CRICKHOWELL
(SO 217 183)

At the beginning of the nineteenth century the traveller and antiquarian Richard Fenton visited Crickhowell and declared it to be 'the most cheerful-looking town I ever saw'; and in the mellow days of spring or summer, that sentiment may well be echoed by latter-day visitors to this market town on the Usk. Of the half dozen or so pubs and inns here, only three need to be singled out.

A few years before Fenton's stay, Sir Richard Colt-Hoare warned visitors that 'there is a tolerable little Inn at the Bear, but a large party cannot be accommodated', which is rather hard to believe since the Bear Inn is one of the largest buildings in the town. In any case, Sir Richard's account may be biased, since he was peeved to find that he had arrived too late for the salmon fishing season. Georgian gripes notwithstanding, the Bear today has an Egon Ronay recommendation, and the Good Pub Guide deems it to be one of the most popular Welsh entries. It is a tall, bland building with a rendered eighteenth-century façade, dotted with long sash windows. Through the arched entrance at the side, horses and coaches once passed to shelter in the rear yard. The interior is large and spacious with a heavy, dark beamed ceiling, hacked for plaster. The craze for covering up 'unsightly' woodwork has long passed, and the dark beauty of the ceiling has been restored to its original state. Beside the elegant wainscoted bar is a large black timber dresser groaning under the weight of pewter mugs and brass plates. In the shadows beneath crouches a ceramic cat, so lifelike it can fool anyone after a pint or two.

As its name suggests, the Bridge End Inn stands at the foot of the hill below the town, guarding the approach over the bridge. It is now awkwardly sited in a fork of the road, but only the east branch is original, and leads past the modest castle ruins and into the heart of the town. When the new bypass road was constructed the builders found it necessary to lengthen the bridge, hence the odd numbered arches – twelve on one side, thirteen on the other. The interior of the pub has been extensively restored in keeping with its old character, but plenty of aged timber and exposed stonework remains, and there is a real fire in one of the three lounges.

The little hexagonal cottage at one end of the pub is an old toll house, where money was levied on all traffic crossing into town. Such buildings were once numerous in the Welsh countryside and many can still be found alongside the old turnpike roads, albeit minus their gates blocking the way. The extortionate tolls proved a heavy burden on the poor, and eventually provoked a series of uprisings in the 1830s and '40s, when the Merched Becca gangs roamed the countryside smashing the hated gates.

Another relic of that period is a plaque on the wall of the White Hart just outside town on the road to Brecon; this lists all the various tolls once paid to the Duke of Beaufort for the passage of vehicles and animals through his gates. The pub itself is not, unfortunately, of fifteenth-century vintage (as the sign claims), but a pleasant eighteenth-century building which was formerly a toll house and cottage.

At a time when each pub brewed its own beer, a good supply of water was essential, and here an adjacent mountain stream was a handy source. In the stream bed can be seen the remains of a dam which was used to channel off water into the brewhouse.

Crickhowell lies 5 miles north-west of Abergavenny, on the A40 road to Brecon. Bear Inn: Bar snacks and meals, accommodation. Open 11 a.m.–3 p.m., 6–11 p.m.

Ashbridge Inn, CWMBRAN
(ST 297 974)

A new and welcome arrival to Cwmbran. Until 1991 the Ashbridge was a nondescript, run-down farmstead, hidden from the road by a screen of bushes; but now, following an extensive programme of work, few passers-by can miss the renovated buildings standing in impressive isolation, and encircled by lawns, gardens and car-parks. The plush interior is enormous, with rooms opening off rooms, several dining areas and lounges, and a separate family room with children's play area. Some of the old outbuildings which formerly stood in the courtyard have been incorporated into the pub, which explains the size. The original farm was never so roomy!

Many of the early features have unfortunately been swept away during the renovation work, and little of the homely farmhouse atmosphere remains. Here and there a few old beams have survived, and some token areas of bare stone wall provide a nice contrast with the elegant wallpaper. Some three centuries ago the Ashbridge was a small and simple farmhouse built to a plan shared by many Gwent houses, including the Royal Oak, Llantrisant (p. 52) and the Ship, Raglan (p. 69). This now forms part of the dining area and children's room, and can be recognized by its lower beamed ceiling. At a later date a large barn was added to one end of the house, and this spacious chamber (bereft of its loft and with a few intrusive modern timbers) forms a most attractive dining room in which to sample the varied menu.

The pub lies beside the A4051 at Pontnewydd, on the way from Cwmbran to Pontypool, M4 junction 26. Bar snacks and meals. Open 11.30–11p.m.; Sunday: 12–10 p.m.

The Star, DINAS POWIS
(ST 153 712)

An unpretentious exterior hides a gem of a Tudor local. Although the nearby Three Horseshoes looks like the oldest pub here, the Star is in fact the most venerable building in Dinas Powis. Only the crumbling castle in the valley below is its senior. It was built during either the reign of Henry VIII or his son and successor, Edward, at a time when the humbler medieval houses in lowland Glamorgan were increasingly being rebuilt in more durable materials.

Dinas Powis, the Star: reconstruction of the hall, *c.* 1550. Apart from the ornate cross-beam ceiling the interior is typical of early Glamorgan houses, with a narrow winding stair beside the main fireplace. The entrance passage was beyond the arched door, although this is no longer part of the pub

From the outside there is nothing to indicate its age, but the Old Court next door has a fine arched entrance, and a row of tiny windows marking the position of a winding stair. These are not two separate houses, but actually the same one; the Court was the kitchen of the original house, while the pub was the adjoining hall. The bar-lounge is an impressive room with a carved stone inglenook, a monumental cross-beam ceiling, and an arched door leading to the winding stairs. Behind the bar can just be seen a recess which marks the site of the original entrance from the kitchen; this was blocked up when the building was split in two. More recent alterations include the construction of an adjoining lounge and restaurant wing. According to legend the inn was used as a court-house during the sixteenth century, and criminals awaiting their fate would be transported along a secret passage below ground, to a grim prison on the other side of the road.

Dinas Powis village lies about 3 miles south-west of Cardiff, on the A4055 to Barry. It can also be reached via the A4050, M4 junction 33. Bar snacks and meals, accommodation. Open 11.30 a.m.–3 p.m., 5.30–11 p.m.

Laleston Inn, LALESTON

(SS 874 800)

Visitors passing through the little village of Laleston on the road to Bridgend cannot fail to notice the magnificent Great House, a sixteenth- and seventeenth-century mansion complete with rows of mullioned windows, bare stonework and clusters of chimneys. After years of dereliction it has been lovingly restored, and is now a restaurant; were it a pub it would have pride of place in this book.

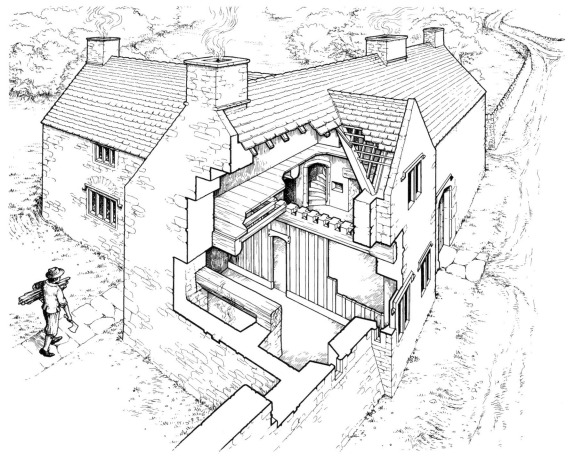

Laleston, Laleston Inn: this cutaway view shows the inn *c.* 1650, when the original two-room lobby-entry house had been extended. The ground-floor partition has now been removed, but the impressive storeyed bay at the front remains. The cutaway wall in the foreground is all that remains of an older building

There is, however, another relic of old Laleston which certainly warrants an entry here. Follow Wind Street up the hill past the medieval church to where, on the right, stands the Laleston Inn and Grey Lady restaurant. The grey lady herself is said to be a former owner of the inn who now haunts the premises, though it is an epithet which could well be applied to the building itself. The plain limestone walls were raised in the last years of the reign of Queen Elizabeth I, at a time when the nearby Great House was also being refurbished. There was an earlier building on the site of the inn, and part of a wall with blocked doors and windows can be seen alongside the car-park.

Dominating the front of the inn is a rare storeyed bay with all its dressed stone windows intact, including even tiny side loops – perhaps for spying out the unwelcome approach of a tax man? Such a wealth of carved stonework in what was originally a small yeoman's farmhouse is unusual, and it may not be far-fetched to assume that the builder was 'keeping up with the Joneses' in an attempt to imitate the splendours of Great House. Inside there is a long, low room (now the bar) with a log fire in a large inglenook. A second fireplace in the opposite wall is almost hidden by mugs, bottles and glittering brassware. This duplication of fireplaces is not inexplicable, for if you look at the central ceiling beam, you will see a row of slots which once held the vertical timbers of a partition dividing this room into a hall and parlour.

Sometime in the latter part of the seventeenth century a large kitchen and bake-house wing was added to the rear, and this part now houses the restaurant. Like the hall this room has a large fireplace with stone winding stairs leading to the upper floor. If the size of a commodious bread-oven is anything to go by, then the cooks produced some hefty loaves here 300 years ago!

The pub lies behind Laleston church off the A4106 Bridgend to Porthcawl road, M4 junctions 36 or 37. Bar snacks and meals. Open 12–3 p.m., 7–11 p.m.

The Skirrid Inn, LLANFIHANGEL CRUCORNEY

(SO 326 207)

Llanfihangel Crucorney is a peaceful little village mercifully bypassed by the A465 Abergavenny to Hereford road. Ample signposts prevent any motorist from missing the place, and there is even a large sign proclaiming the presence of the Skirrid Inn, which has gained itself the almost-official title of the oldest hostelry in Wales.

The village stands on a hilltop where the river Honddu emerges from the hills around Llanthony Priory. Everywhere you look there are ruggedly plain stone walls spotted with lichen and moss; modern stucco and pebbledash has yet to disfigure the village-scape at Llanfihangel. The parish church of St Michael is one of the oddities of the village; half is roofed, the remainder open to the elements. Tower Farm, opposite the Post Office, has a bizarre castellated folly attatched to one end of the building.

Plainest and most rugged of all is the Skirrid Inn, and the almost overwhelming grimness of the façade is only just lightened by the spacious wooden mullioned windows. Above the windows is a series of stone relieving arches which provide something in the way of decoration to contrast with the bare masonry. But these arches pose a question – if they were meant to provide structural support, then why are they not centrally placed over the openings? The answer, of course, is that the existing windows are modifications, and originally there would have been six smaller windows equally spaced around a central doorway.

And what a theatrical prop is that door – a dark and heavy mass of oak studded with nails and cross bars. It is too well oiled to creak when you open it, but it should; for it all adds to the atmosphere of this haunted house. There are more ghostly goings-on, folk-tales, grisly deaths and unspoken secrets connected with the Skirrid than any other pub in Wales. Even before customers enter the building the sign on the cobbled forecourt displays one miraculous event, a lightning bolt striking the Skirrid mountain and splitting it asunder. Local folklore, however, claims that the huge landslip on one side of the nearby peak was caused by an earthquake at the time of the Crucifixion. And there is the stone mounting block from which Owain Glyndwr is said to have rallied his native troops during the rebellion of 1400–12. These, like many of the stories concerning the Skirrid, hinge on its reputation as the oldest pub in Wales. It is claimed that the inn was here in 1110, when a local man was tried for the heinous crime of sheep stealing. He was hanged from a beam under the great stair. A further 180 victims of rough justice are said to have shared his fate, and that beam is now gouged and disfigured by the marks of countless ropes.

Treading a cautious path between fact and fiction, it would be best to say that such stories may very well relate to an earlier building on this site, but all the architectural details firmly indicate a seventeenth-century date for the existing inn. The Gwent artist and historian, Fred Hando, pointed this out more than thirty years ago, yet many guidebooks still stress the imaginary age of the building. But this demolition of a long-cherished belief should not be an occasion for grief; quite the opposite, for the Skirrid Inn is an excellent example of a Renaissance centrally-planned gentry house. It was built at a time when those rich enough to construct large houses were adopting the concepts brought about by the revival of Classical architecture. The old medieval-type dwellings, centred on the hall, were giving way to more symmetrical houses with several rooms of equal importance, grouped about a central passage and stairway. With such a plan there was a far greater degree

Llanfihangel Crucorney, the Skirrid Inn: although the front has a more impressive façade, this cutaway view c. 1680 through the back of the inn, shows the typical Renaissance-inspired plan of rear service rooms linked to a main stairway for maximum privacy and circulation. The size and complexity of the stair can well be appreciated from this view

of privacy and better circulation; servants could cross through the house and pass up and down stairs without actually entering any of the main rooms.

A customer entering the Skirrid in the seventeenth century would have stood in a wide and lofty passageway, with doors at the opposite end leading to the rear kitchen and stair. The hall lay to the left of the passage, and the parlour on the right. The monumental oak staircase climbed past the first-floor guest chambers to the attic, where some servants probably slept. Though there have been some inevitable changes, partitions taken down, new doors and windows provided and some rooms modernized, much of the Skirrid remains as it was built (or, to give the legends their due, rebuilt) in the reign of Charles I. The hall is still the same, with its deep stone fireplace, and lofty ceiling cross-beamed with carved timbers. Finest of all the surviving features is the staircase, 'where delicacy and refinement are wedded to strength and dignity' as Hando observed. All the timberwork has warped and settled into interesting shapes over the years, but despite the uneven boards and frequent creaks the whole latticework is as sound today as it was when a nameless craftsman completed it over 350 years ago.

Halfway up between the ground and first floors is a low door leading into a small room, where condemned felons spent their last night before sentence was carried out. That the Skirrid Inn was used as a court-house by the Circuit Judge is undisputed, although inevitably this has led to claims that the notorious Judge Jeffreys stayed here. Having passed sentence of death on some miserable miscreant, the judge would retire to his comfortable chamber on the first floor, while the condemned man waited in his lonely little room for a quick drop down the stairwell the following morning.

Echoes of those unpleasant days still trouble some visitors to the inn. One guest was physically unable to climb the stairs beyond the small room, as if held back by an invisible hand. Another had a choking fit at dinner, and on leaving the inn her companion noticed a red mark around her throat – like a rope burn. An unwelcome guest is the ghost of a one-eyed convict, who stabbed himself to death in his cell to cheat the hangman. These and other tales are mentioned in various newspaper articles displayed on the walls of the bar. Several old manuscripts discovered during renovation work here a few years ago, have also been framed. One fragment is from a wage book of 1680, while another is a bill for 4*s* 10*d* charged to Squire Arnold of nearby Llanfihangel Court. This squire was a nasty piece of work, and it was probably his ruthless hunting of local Catholics during the Popish Plot of 1679 that gave rise to the story of Judge Jeffrey's presence here.

One final thread deserves to be singled out from this rich tapestry of fact and fiction; above the great fireplace in the hall is a small stone shelf on which, in days gone by, the landlord would place a jug of ale every night. The recipient of this free gift was an unseen and unwelcome guest, but an ever-present one – the Devil!

The Skirrid is signposted off the A465 Abergavenny to Hereford road, about 4 miles north-east of Abergavenny. Bar snacks and meals, accommodation. Open 12–3 p.m., 7–11 p.m.

The White Hart, LLANGYBI
(ST 373 966)

Llangybi is a little village clustered about the Usk to Caerleon road, a delight for the seeker of the picturesque, but a frustrating obstacle for any motorist loath to travel at less than 40 miles an hour. The road snakes its way up, down and around the village; even the medieval parish church seems to be hiding down the hillside out of the way of all the noise and bustle. A screen of ancient yews further adds to its camouflaged retreat.

At the centre of Llangybi is the village green, a little patch of grass neatly encircled by roads and completely overshadowed by the spreading canopy of a great oak. A metal bench surrounds the ivy-covered trunk, providing visitors with a shady resting place from which to view the White Hart. Few travellers can miss the inn as they pass through Llangybi, for it stands on a sharp bend, with eye-achingly bright whitewashed walls.

According to popular tradition the origin of the inn is linked to the nearby church, which reputedly was founded in the sixth century by St Cybi. At the side of a lane opposite the churchyard wall is a trickling spring which is blessed with the saint's name, and which is believed to have been created when the thirsty Cybi stuck his staff into the ground. However, the legends of Cybi's arrival in Wales and the miraculous spring is more strongly associated with Anglesey in North Wales; and so the church here on the banks of the Usk was probably established by followers of the saint rather than the holy man himself. Similarly, the belief that the church formed part of a monastery and that the inn was built to house the monks has little foundation in truth. A variant of this tale claims that the White Hart was a guest-house owned by the Knights Hospitallers of St John, a military brethren established to protect pilgrims in the Holy Land.

Perhaps these stories came about through an attempt to link the name of the inn to the white habits worn by Cistercian monks; be that as it may, a careful study of the building will reveal no architectural details which could be pre-Reformation. The plain stone walls, sagging roofline, low timber windows and clustered diagonal chimney stacks, all help to give the building a look of great age; but ignoring the tenacious grip of tradition, the evidence points to an early seventeenth-century date, and it was probably built in the closing years of the reign of 'Good Queen Bess'.

The plan alone is particularly interesting, and before entering the pub customers can see that it consists of two largely similar blocks, set at right angles to each other, but joined at one corner. Both blocks have been lengthened by the addition of a cottage and a stable at either end. The interiors are largely similar, with low beamed ceilings, winding stairs to the upper floors and attics, and the entrance alongside the inglenooks.

The earliest part of the building is the east block, now the bar, which faces the main road. The adjoining wing was added a generation or two later; there was enough of a lapse between building phases for there to be slightly different finishes to the decorations. The unusual plan of the White Hart places it in the 'unit system' group of houses, where two or more self-contained dwellings occupy the same courtyard. No one is quite sure why some sites developed in this fashion (examples are known of up to four little houses in a single group) but some of the units were bakehouses or servants' quarters, and others were dower houses – where the widow of a householder would live, while the heir and his family dwelt in the 'big house'. The second house at the White Hart was evidently a status symbol as well as containing the best chambers for the owner and his family. The plaster ceiling of the first-floor chamber and the wall above the fireplace are covered with a variety of decorations including Tudor roses, fleurs-de-lis, horses' heads, and either a flower or a thistle. Could the latter be a reference to the badge of Scotland, suggesting that the house was decorated in the reign of James I?

'Some years ago,' wrote Fred Hando in the 1950s, 'a few of us saved the White Hart from desecration. A great beam from the fireplace had been removed in readiness for the introduction of a modern atrocity. Fortunately some enlightened directors stepped in at the right moment and saved a sixteenth-century relic.' If Hando was referring to the tree trunk above the hall fireplace, then it must have taken a gargantuan effort to remove such a chunk of wood in the first place! The local blacksmith also volunteered the information that three cobblers used to work up in the attic; which is not so unlikely as it may sound, since many old houses had sleeping chambers for servants in the roof space. Here the large dormer window provided plenty of light, and the projecting gable chimneys show that both attics were heated – a rare luxury indeed!

Llangybi, the White Hart: the cutaway reconstruction of the inn clearly shows the original plan of two self-contained houses side by side. Both buildings are virtually identical, although the older house (at front) belongs to the hearth-passage group, while the rear has a lobby-entrance

The inn is reputedly haunted by the ghostly form of a woman flitting about the upper rooms, and there is said to be a secret passage leading to the church. Surprisingly there is still some sort of tunnel here, which very probably gave rise to the 'secret passage' story. Behind the unusually deep fireplace in the lounge there is a low, dark passage with a short flight of stone steps leading down to an opening about 1½ ft square. This apparently once connected with the outside, but was blocked up when the adjoining stable was built in the nineteenth century. What this was used for is a mystery. Could it have been a source of light and air for a priest's hole hidden behind the fireplace? Or was it an uncomfortable exit for smugglers or criminals wishing to leave the White Hart without drawing the attention of the forces of Law and Order?

One early customer of the inn certainly drew attention to himself in a spectacular way, as a framed newspaper cutting of 1855 reveals. In May of that year one Richard Daniel caused a rumpus by 'indecently exposing his person' to all and sundry. The Victorian flasher was hauled before the petty sessions at Caerleon where the judge was presented with conflicting evidence; some claimed Richard had revealed all, others said he hadn't. Although presented with the bare facts, the judge was unable to get to the bottom of the affair but still sent the unfortunate flasher to the local workhouse.

Customers of the White Hart are today spared another unsettling sight; anyone entering the pub has to pass along a corridor between the old hall and a nineteenth-century cottage before turning into the bar. Before the cottage was built this passage was, of course, part of the courtyard, over which passed a footpath and right-of-way to the church. You can still see the stile in the graveyard wall directly opposite the rear door. Image the sobering effect when early customers were confronted with a grim procession of clergy, mourners and coffin bearers, passing along this right-of-way through the pub, on their way to a burial service at the church!

Llangybi village lies on a minor road from Caerleon to Usk, M4 junction 25. Bar snacks and meals. Open 11 a.m.–3 p.m., 6–11 p.m.

The Old House, LLANGYNWYD
(SS 857 887)

The Old House Inn comes as a pleasant surprise to anyone who believes that thatching is a feature found only in England or lowland Wales. This mountain-top inn seems to hide from the visitor in a tree-shaded hollow below the village street. A tiny dormer window peeps out from beneath the thatch like a sleepy, half-opened eye. Within, jugs and mugs hang from blackened seventeenth-century beams. A typical Glamorgan fireplace with stone winding stairs occupies the whole width of one wall, and above the oak lintel a long mirror reflects a glittering array of brass ornaments.

The original Old House was very small, just the area of the present bar, but extension work in the eighteenth and nineteenth centuries greatly enlarged the accommodation – so much so that the adjoining restaurant was once used as a Nonconformist meeting place! More recently a larger restaurant and lounge area have been added to one side of the seventeenth-century house, with spacious windows offering diners views across the Bryncynan valley.

In the yard outside a creaking signpost depicts the 'Mari Lwyd' calling at the pub. This bizarre procession, comprising a small group of revellers headed by Mari – a horse's skull draped with a white cloth and ribbons – was once a common sight in nineteenth-century Glamorgan and Gwent at the Calennig (New Year) festivities. The Mari called at each house in the village, and the bearer would sing a verse inviting the occupant to join in a form of contest. It was up to the householder to reply in the same metre to each verse sung by the revellers, and if they failed, then the boisterous procession would enter and help themselves to the food and drink invariably provided! Various students have put forward theories explaining the origins of the Mari Lwyd ritual; one

Llangynwyd, the Old House: the Mari Lwyd shown on the sign

of the least unlikely is that it may be the sole remnant of a medieval mystery play, acted out long after the rest of the play was forgotten. The name, incidentally, translates as the 'grey mare'. The Llangynwyd Mari can be seen on display at the Welsh Folk Museum, St Fagans, near Cardiff.

As in many rural villages, pride of place at Llangynwyd is reserved for the parish church which stands opposite the inn. On a modern granite cross beside the churchyard are engraved the names of Wil Hopcyn (1701–41) and Ann Thomas (1704–27), the Maid of Cefn Ydfa. Though the mansion of Cefn Ydfa is now a ruin, the story of the ill-fated lovers has proved to be one of the most enduring romances of Glamorgan, and has secured Llangynwyd a place on the folk-tale map of Wales. Pictures, articles and genealogies displayed within the pub serve to remind all customers of this legend which, however, is vociferously believed by many to be true.

Wil, a local labourer and poet, was deeply in love with Ann Thomas, the only child of a moderately wealthy family. Their love was mutual, but Ann's domineering mother had no inclination to see her daughter mixing with the lower classes and intended her to marry a well-to-do neighbour, Anthony Maddocks. Barred from meeting his beloved, the disconsolate Wil turned to poetry, and wrote (allegedly at the inn) the poignant song '*Bugeilio'r Gwenith Gwyn*':

Myfi sydd fachgen ifanc ffol,   A simple youthful lad am I,
Yn caru'n ol fy ffansi;   who loves at fancy's pleasure;
Mi yn bugeilio'r gwenith gwyn,   I fondly watch the blooming wheat,
Ac arall yn ei fedi.   but another reaps the treasure.

Despite being locked in her room Ann managed to smuggle out love letters with her maid's connivance. When her mother found out and removed all ink and paper, Ann wrote messages with her own blood on a sycamore leaf.

But the marriage went ahead. Ann pined, Wil grieved, and Maddocks counted his gains. Time passed. Then one day, Wil (who had moved to Bristol in search of work) had a dream that Maddocks had died. He rushed back to the mountain village only to find that it was Ann who was dying, and she passed away in his arms while the feckless husband was out hunting.

Llangynwyd village lies 1¹/₂ miles south of Maesteg town. From M4 junction 36, follow the A4063 through Tondu to Maesteg, for 5 miles. A signposted turning for Llangynwyd church will be seen on the left. Bar snacks and meals. Open 11 a.m.–11 p.m., winter: 11 a.m.–4 p.m., 6–11 p.m.

The Royal Oak, LLANTRISANT
(ST 391 969)

One of the delightful villages in the vale of Usk bypassed (for better rather than worse) by the A449, though the roar of the traffic can still disturb the peace on occasion. The church 'of the three saints' stands beside a stream in the village, while the only other building of any historical note is the Royal Oak itself – tall, imposing, an immaculately kept whitewashed building crowning a knoll beside the road. There is a large parking area, a front garden and patio area overlooking the valley. Some adjoining buildings have been converted into guest rooms supplementing the accommodation at the inn itself. In plan the Royal Oak is identical to another Usk valley pub, the Ship at Raglan (p. 69). There is a large hall, heavy with blackened beams, a lost inner room (only the slots on the beams mark the removed partition) and another large room behind the inglenook which was once a parlour or kitchen, but is now an elegant lounge. A later wing at the rear forms an extension to the bar. This house was built at a time of increasing prosperity for the owner, for not only were there spacious rooms on the first floor, but also in the attic, reached by a large wooden stair. All the architectural details indicate a late seventeenth-century date, and so, unfortunately, the traditional medieval origin of the Royal Oak must be consigned to folklore.

Llantrisant lies in the Usk valley between Newport and Usk. The best way to reach it is via a signposted minor road from Usk town to Newbridge. Alternatively, from Caerleon (M4 junction 25) follow the signposted minor road to Llangybi and Usk, and take the right turn by Cwrt Bleddyn country hotel. Follow this through Newbridge, over the river, and to Llantrisant after 2 miles. Bar meals, accommodation. Open 6–11 p.m.

LLANTWIT MAJOR
(SS 967 687)

The village of Llantwit (and ultimately its pubs) owes its origins to missionary zeal of Dark Age saints and holy men. Over fifteen centuries ago the Word of God was spread through the Welsh countryside by men such as Dewi, Cadoc, Teilo and Illtud, and it was the latter who founded an ecclesiastical 'college' here on the banks of the Ogney brook, just over a mile inland from the sea.

Even today Llantwit retains abundant signs of its long ecclesiastical history. There is the large and imposing parish church, a ruined medieval chantry house beside the graveyard, and on the hill to the west are the remains of a monastic grange which belonged to Tewkesbury Abbey. Within the church are several Early Christian memorial stones, including a magnificent decorated cross in memory of King Hywel, a vassal of Alfred the Great.

Almost any road the visitor takes to reach Llantwit passes some noble house of long-departed families; there is ruined Boverton Place to the east, and equally defunct Old Place off West Street. High Street passes within the shadow of Great House, a multi-gabled Elizabethan mansion rescued from decay in the 1940s. Llantwit was not a planned settlement, and the streets and houses were left to grow into a tangle on the hillside above the brook and the brooding church. The village 'square' is, in fact, a triangular intersection of roads beside the sixteenth-century town hall. A stone plinth topped with a modern memorial cross forms a pleasing obstacle in the middle, and grouped about it are three ancient pubs – the Old White Hart, the Tudor Tavern, and the Old Swan Inn.

The Swan is by far the finest of the three, a great, grey mass of locally quarried limestone, besprinkled with carved sandstone doors and windows. There is no mistaking the antiquity of this building, nor is there a thick coat of rendering or whitewash to disguise the rugged beauty of the clean-washed stonework. Thankfully plastic or metal double-glazed casements have not replaced the original arched stone windows. If time is not pressing, then any customer of the Swan should read a small booklet chronicling the known and conjectured history of the inn, which was written by the landlord (who is also the chef, an amateur artist and a local historian). The inevitable tales of secret passages can be discounted, but there is a glimmer of truth in the story that the inn was used as a mint by the monks, since brass trade tokens were cast here during the Civil War.

One of the more interesting theories mentioned in the booklet claims that the Swan was originally a medieval longhouse, and that cattle used to be tethered in one room while the occupants lived in another. The upper floor was supposedly reached by an outside stone stair, which was afterwards roofed over and incorporated into the building when the rear kitchen wing was added. It is an attractive theory, but there is little architectural evidence to support it and it would be best to rely on the opinion of the Royal Commission on Ancient and Historical Monuments which places a late sixteenth-century date on the building. The Swan was probably constructed towards the end of Queen Elizabeth's reign, at a time when there was an upsurge in building in lowland Glamorgan. Doubtless it replaced a more humble dwelling. In any case, all the surviving details (Tudor arched doors, carved stone windows, and heavy chamfered beams) are shared by many Llantwit houses and confirm the sixteenth-century date. More unusual is the storeyed bay which projects out into the street. The large windows would have lit the high table where the moderately well-to-do owner sat with his family at mealtimes. That person may have been the estate bailiff of the Raglan family, and the aforementioned guidebook also identifies the Swan as the home of Hopkin ap Rhys.

This otherwise undistinguished character played a cameo role in a dramatic and violent episode in Llantwit history. By the late sixteenth century the two main gentry families of the district were the Seys of Boverton House and the Vans of Old Place, and the rivalry which existed between them exploded in bloodshed one October Sunday morning in 1597. Richard Sey and his family were already inside the church and the service had either started, or was about to begin, when Edmund Van and his retinue burst in. 'Sirrah, thou are a saucy Jacke, that is not thy place,' cried Edmund, and beat up an elderly servant of the Seys who was at prayer in a pew. Peace was restored, but as soon as the service finished the Van gang rushed outside to lie in wait. When the Seys emerged they faced a ring of armed men. The execrable Edmund then pushed Richard's pregnant wife to the ground, and threatened to stab her, but the group managed to break away and run up the hill.

A huge commotion then ensued as the armed Vans chased after the unarmed Seys, until the beleaguered party managed to reach the comparative safety of Hopkin's house, presumably the Swan Inn. And not a moment too soon, for Edmund and his gang arrived and 'did presentlie with all violence assault and seeke in very forcible manner to breake open the dores and windowes of the said howse, that they might have entraunce thereunto and thereby mischeif the said Mr Seys and his companie'. But the stout wooden doors and small windows defeated their purposes, and when the parish constable bravely tried to intervene he was set upon, and only just escaped with his life to a neighbouring cottage. The gang then turned their attentions elsewhere, running riot through the narrow streets, and sending the village folk fleeing for their lives crying, 'see your dores be fast, they are coming!' It was not until later that day that peace returned to Llantwit, when Sir Edward Stradling of St Donats Castle rode into the village, with a large group of loyal followers, and escorted the terrified Seys back to their mansion. Edmund Van was later imprisoned and fined for his actions, although his monstrous egotism led him to say that if the constable ever again dared to interfere in his 'right' to

Llantwit Major, the Old Swan: this reconstruction shows the inn during the riot of 1597. Part of the storeyed bay window (on the right) has been cut away to show the first-floor fireplace

start a riot, then he would end up 'far worser than before'. This illuminating episode of Elizabethan gentry pastimes was recorded by the local author John Stradling, Sir Edward's kinsman and heir.

On a more pleasant note the Swan has also catered for more sedate and illustrious guests, particularly when the old Stradling stronghold of St Donats was purchased by the American tycoon, William Randolph Hearst, in 1925. Hearst refurbished the crumbling castle as a luxurious holiday home and invited over many of his Hollywood friends, including Marion Davies, Sammy Davies Jnr and

Bette Davis. A string of big cars would ferry the guests from the castle to the Old Swan, where a side room was reserved for their use. Prime Ministers Neville Chamberlain and Winston Churchill have also visited the Swan.

The Swan was also the resting place of the circuit judge and his retinue, while staying in Llantwit to dispense rough justice in the town hall across the road. Wrongdoers awaiting their fate were locked in the dark and damp medieval cellars below the sixteenth-century building. Just beside the court-house stands the Tudor Tavern, probably of slightly later date than the Swan, and now engulfed in a terrace of more recent buildings. The interior has been extensively altered and the original ceiling beams replaced with pale imitations, but a fine Tudor doorway remains behind the juke-box.

Across the road is the Old White Hart, living up to its name with dazzlingly bright whitewashed walls. It was built around the same time as its venerable neighbour, the Swan, although the coated walls and modern windows help to disguise its age. The interior too has unfortunately been deprived of its original heavy timber-beamed ceiling – the crowning feature of many old pubs. But there are other features to admire here; the inglenook with its crooked beam, the blocked winding stairs (soon to be reopened) and the varying shapes of the door-heads, indicating different dates of construction. The pub is claimed to be haunted by the ghost of a lonely old man who died in an asylum, but you may have better luck at spotting architectural details than elusive phantoms.

Llantwit lies near the coast in the Vale of Glamorgan, about 4 miles south of Cowbridge. The village can be reached via the B4270, or along the B4265 from either Bridgend or Barry.Bar snacks and meals. Open 11.30 a.m.–11 p.m.

Plough and Harrow, MONKNASH
(SS 919 706)

Needless to say, with a name like Monknash there is a strong ecclesiastical background to the origin of this small Vale village. Local tradition claims that there was a monastery here, and that the Plough and Harrow formed part of it; but in fact Monknash was a grange – an outlying farm established by a monastery to provide food and other goods. In that function it differed little from any other secular farm, though there was usually a chapel on site, and the estate was run by lay-brothers, the 'draught oxen of God' as one unflattering chronicler put it.

Monknash, the Plough and Harrow: the seventeenth-century part of the building is to the right of the porch

The monks' grange at Nash (hence the place-name) was the richest estate owned by the Cistercian abbey at Neath, but with the downfall of monastic houses in 1536, the land was sold off to the wealthy Stradling family of St Donats Castle. Even today the remains of that monastic farm are quite substantial, with the earthworks of roads, boundaries and buildings in the fields behind the pub. More impressive is a stone dovecot, and a huge tithe barn, over 200 ft long, a building so large that the porch alone now accommodates a modern house!

The pub's name is particularly apt too, considering the intense agricultural activity carried out here by the monastic servants over 450 years ago. Although not as old as the grange, the Plough and Harrow is still a respectable three and a half centuries old, and it was probably built during the reign of King James I. A walled walkway sweeps the visitor up to the front door; open it, and you face a blank wall! This is an example of a 'lobby entry' house; turn right and you enter the bar, with its beamed ceiling, 'Tudor' doors and sooty inglenook. This is now one large room, and all traces have been removed of a partitioned-off chamber which stood at the far end. Perhaps this is a good thing, for there is a gruesome tradition that this room was used to store shipwrecked bodies before they were taken to the nearby church for burial.

The village of Monknash lies about 3 miles north-west of Llantwit Major, and can be reached from the M4 at junction 35. Follow the dual carriageway to Bridgend, and at the third roundabout take the signposted turning to St Brides Major (B4265). About 1½ miles beyond St Brides a signposted right turn leads to Monknash and Llantwit. Bar meals. Open 11 a.m–2 p.m., 6–11 p.m.

The Robin Hood, MONMOUTH
(SO 507 128)

The historic county town of Monmouth has its fair share of famous sons and distinguished visitors; the first was Geoffrey of Monmouth, the twelfth-century writer who brought to life the legendary exploits of King Arthur. Then in 1387 Henry V was born in the grim Norman castle on the hill above the town. Wordsworth was here in 1793 and 1798, and in 1802 Monmouth played host to Nelson and Lady Hamilton. Charles Stewart Rolls, the pioneering motorist and aviator, lived here, and his statue stands in the narrow market square, overlooked by a curiously twisted effigy of Henry (which is more reminiscent of Richard III than the victor of Agincourt). For some unknown reason another medieval hero has arrived in Monmouth, and at the lower end of Monnow Street, where the road narrows to cross the magnificent fortified bridge, there stands the Robin Hood inn.

This is claimed to be the oldest pub in town, and the dressed stone Tudor arch doorway is an obvious indicator of age. The walls were probably built around the beginning of the sixteenth-century, but all the carved beams and timber partitions inside date to the late seventeenth century, when the inn was completely remodelled. At about the same time the upper half of the front wall was demolished and replaced with a half-timbered façade, and the main room on the first floor graced with a decorative plaster ceiling. This room is the showpiece of the inn, and the owner was clearly intent on keeping up with the latest fashion in decor. The fruit motif which dominates the ceiling also appears in Great House, built on the site of the castle in 1673, and which was probably the inspiration for the Robin Hood design.

In the days when the Catholic faith was viewed by many as disruptive and seditious, persecuted believers would secretly gather in the upper room to celebrate Mass. Some fifteen years after the first Catholic Relief Act was passed by parliament in 1778, the local council agreed to allow the building of a 'Publick Catholic Chapel' in Monmouth, but demanded that it should not look like a chapel, and that it had to be located out of sight behind some houses! The person who financed the building was Michael Watkins, proprietor of the inn which for so long had sheltered the beleaguered worshippers.

The Robin Hood is thought to have been an inn for centuries, though it may only have received its present name in the eighteenth century, when a sign outside carried the verse:

> Walk in kind sirs, my ale is good,
> and take a pot with Robin Hood;
> If Robin Hood is not at home
> Pray take a pot with Little John.

Fred Hando recalled the strong tradition that Shakespeare visited Monmouth and stayed here: 'scorn my conjecture if you will, but in my mind the light relief in his *Henry V* savours of the Robin Hood taproom.' Certainly there are plenty of references in the play to Monmouth, and the Gwent sprite Pwcca reappears as Puck in *A Midsummer Night's Dream*, but like many of the stories concerning the widely-travelled bard, there is little real evidence to back up such claims.

For long, no one could be quite sure if Monmouth and its shire belonged to Wales or England, hence the frequent absence of the county from earlier guidebooks on Wales. Like Usk and Abergavenny, the town has a long and eventful history; originally founded by the Romans, then settled and fortified by the Normans, the town has continued to grow beyond the limits of the medieval walls, so that the few remains of its architectural heritage are continually at risk. The much photographed Monnow bridge with its fortified gatehouse (the only one now surviving in Britain) is particularly under threat from twentieth-century traffic. The town walls have long gone, but one of the two round towers which straddled the east gate still remains, incorporated into the otherwise modern Nag's Head in St James Street. Lower down the street, at the corner of Wyebridge Street, stands the Queen's Head, a rambling timber-framed building of *c.* 1630, which was extensively restored in 1922. All the external timberwork is modern, but is said to repeat the original pattern discovered under the plain rendered walls during restoration. Some of the original features still remain inside, however, including a post and panel partition alongside the lobby, and a large inglenook in the bar. One other Monmouth pub deserves a brief mention here, the Vine Tree in Monnow

Street; a dressed stone fireplace in the dining room, and a timber-framed wall in the bar reveal that this outwardly nineteenth-century building is much older. Like so many of the shops and houses in this historic town, the genteel Victorian façades succeed in hiding the uncouth skeletons of their forebears from the gaze of all but the most dedicated and observant researcher.

Monmouth lies in the Wye valley alongside the A40 between Newport and Ross-on-Wye, M50 junction 4, M4 junction 24. Bar snacks and meals. Open 11 a.m.–11 p.m.

Old Murenger House, NEWPORT
(ST 310 883)

This is a splendidly unexpected sight in a city of mostly modern architecture, a gleaming half-timbered black and white sixteenth-century house, hunched between towering blocks, but still dominating the streetscape. Its monochrome glories would not be out of place in one of the border towns such as Ludlow or Chester, where such houses survive in greater numbers; but in the towns and cities of Wales such treasures are, alas, all too rare. Indeed we are fortunate to have this lone relic, for in 1980 the leaning front had started to collapse, and there were fears that it could not be preserved. But conservation work saved the day, and the pub was reopened the following year.

Old Murenger House is something of a misnomer, for the actual dwelling of the murenger (the officer who collected taxes for the upkeep of the town walls) stood elsewhere in Newport, and was apparently demolished in the nineteenth century. In any case the name must be treated with caution since the office of murenger became extinct as far back as 1324, when King Edward II granted the townsfolk a royal charter for the repair of their defences. The castle (and its protective enclave) was founded by the Normans in the late eleventh century as a 'new port' to supplant older Caerleon further up the river Usk. The walls, towers and battlements were built to protect the Anglo-Norman settlers from hostile attack, but since Newport was burnt in 1294, 1316, 1321 and 1402 it would appear that the defences were not particularly efficient. Some authorities believe that only the gates were built in stone, the remainder of the defensive perimeter consisting of a timber palisade.

It would have been a very hardy timber house to have survived such devastating raids, and the existing building was constructed in the more settled years of the Tudor dynasty, when the need for medieval fortifications had passed. It may have been the town house of the wealthy Herbert family of nearby St Julian's Manor, and the traditional date for the building is 1530. There is evidence, however, to suggest that it could have been built some years earlier, for on the upper floor decorative features include the Tudor rose and pineapple badge of Aragon, evidently an acknowledgement of the marriage of Henry VIII to Catherine of Aragon (1509–33).

The exterior elevation is certainly the best part of the house, with jettied upper floors which hang out over the street, seemingly defying gravity. On the ground floor is a broad bay window with leaded panel depicting coats of arms. The interior is, sadly, less impressive. A few blackened beams show, but much is hidden behind plaster and paper.

A modern inscription on one of the beams informs us that the Old Murenger House is the only pub in Wales owned by Samuel Smith, independent Yorkshire brewer, and some framed photos of that brewery seem out of place in this Tudor building. But sit in the bay window with its dark beams and diamond panes, and stare through the thick, milky glass, and you may just catch a fleeting impression of town life in sixteenth-century Newport.

Old Murenger House stands at the top end of High Street, near the railway station in Newport centre, M4 junction 26. Bar meals. Open 11 a.m.–3 p.m., 5.30–11 p.m., Saturday: 11 a.m.–11 p.m.

Baron's Court, PENARTH
(ST 174 727)

Four and a half centuries ago, when Sir George Herbert rebuilt the old manor at Cogan Pill, the house stood on a hillside overlooking the estuaries of the Taff and Ely rivers. Away to the north stretched the coastal plain of Rumney and Wentlooge, backed by the Gwent hills; to the east lay the clifftops of Penarth and, beyond the Bristol Channel, the counties of Avon and Somerset.

That view still remains today, and so does the hall – but how they have changed! The estuary is now spanned by a snaking ribbon of concrete and tarmac – the new bypass road that will soon cross the heart of the proposed Cardiff Bay marina development. The A4055 passes within a few yards of the hall, and has removed every last scrap of rural solitude, and, perhaps the greatest change of all, Cardiff has grown from an insignificant market town into a great, sprawling, ever-expanding city.

Even the name has recently changed, and Sir George's hall is now Baron's Court rather than the older Cogan Pill (the 'pill' is the tidal creek at the foot of the hill). There have been many changes within the building too, and some internal walls have been swept away for a bar extension and an increased restaurant area. But despite these alterations, something of the splendour and great space of the original Tudor hall can be experienced.

There is some uncertainty about the age of the building. It may have been built by Sir Matthew Cradock of Swansea, who had leased the property in the late fifteenth century, or else by his grandson, Sir George Herbert, whose arms are shown above the door. When the antiquarian John Leland visited Cogan in c. 1540 he noted 'a fair Maner Place' here, and so presumably this was the building he saw. We also know that there was a dock below the house, for court records highlight a dramatic incident which took place here two years before Leland's visit. Walter Herbert, a rather nasty piece of work, had seized a ship berthed at the dock, alleging that 'she had not paid her dues, and had on board certain portingales [i.e. Portuguese] who were fleeing justice in their own country'. The unfortunate captain of the ship was 'locked up . . . without mete or drinke', although most of the refugees managed to escape. One woman, however, died in unknown circumstances in the woods around Cogan. The incarcerated captain was then charged with her murder, and he in turn accused Walter Herbert and his master, the constable of Cardiff Castle, of 'tyrannous behaviour'.

When the inquest was convened the court could only understand what two of the Portuguese witnesses were saying by using an interpreter – who was a servant of Walter Herbert! The records are frustratingly incomplete and do not record the outcome, but we can imagine that wealth and influence counted more than truth and justice in that Tudor court.

The Herberts further enlarged the building around 1550, but by the middle of the following century the family had moved to the Greyfriars in Cardiff, and Cogan Pill became a tenanted farmhouse. It remained in this humble state until around 1851 when it was purchased and restored by J.S. Corbett, a magistrate and agent for the second Marquis of Bute, the founder of modern Cardiff. We have Corbett to thank for saving the building from further decay, although his work included refurbishing the house with many spurious Victorian 'Gothic' features such as battlements and oriel windows. But once the idealism and energy of the late nineteenth century passed, the fortunes of the house took a downward turn; the gardens became rank and overgrown,

Penarth, Baron's Court: cutaway reconstruction of the Tudor hall, *c.* 1540. The lateral chimney and conjectured gallery can be seen, as well as the porch with its heraldic crest. There is evidence to suggest the former existence of a turret (shown right) and there may even have been another wing jutting out from the hall where the figures stand

and many of the interior fittings were sold off. When the house was put on the market in 1965 there was a rumour that residential chalets would be built in the grounds. Mercifully this plan was never carried out, and the medieval hall was opened as a country club. More recently it has been thoroughly refurbished as a Beefeater restaurant and a public house.

Customers now enter Baron's Court through the imposing storeyed porch, which was an architectural status symbol designed to impress upon all the influence and social standing of the owners. A richly carved stone plaque above the door displays the armorial bearings of the Berkeley, Cradock and Herbert families, yet another symbol of Tudor self-pride. Beyond a second door there was a cross-passage separating the great hall from stores and service rooms. This area has now been converted into an elegant restaurant with exposed stonework, arched windows and aged wood in abundance.

At the far end of the passage another door would once have led out into the gardens, but it now opens into the mid-sixteenth-century kitchen wing. Turn right and you enter the hall, the heart of the medieval house, where day-to-day affairs were carried out, and where the family could entertain guests in some luxury. A large fireplace in the side wall provided some heat, and in the day there would have been ample light from the many high windows. The householder and his family would have sat at the far end of hall, probably on a raised platform again to signal their status. On one side of the high table there was a doorway which probably led into a now-destroyed privy turret, while on the opposite side a large archway may have given access to an oriel window overlooking the estuary. The existing window is Victorian, the stones brought from St John's church in the city, but the large pointed arch is apparently original, and pre-dates the Tudor building. Presumably it formed part of the earlier manor house here, and was only discovered again in the course of J.S. Corbett's restoration work.

Decorative timber galleries spanned the width of the hall at either end, one providing access to the chambers over the porch and service rooms. These have now gone, but modern copies provide first-floor diners with an impression of what it would have been like 400 years ago, to look down on all the bustle in the hall as a great banquet or social gathering was being prepared.

Baron's Court lies on the outskirts of Cardiff, at the Llandough-Penarth roundabout on the A4160. The quickest way to reach the pub is from M4 junction 33, along the A4232 to the present terminal roundabout, and then taking the signposted flyover road to Penarth. This road passes the front door of the pub! Bar snacks and meals. Open 11 a.m.–11 p.m.

The Rock and Fountain, PENHOW

(ST 426 910)

'Thou broughtest water for them out of the rock for their thirst,' announces a biblical inscription on the wall of this seventeenth-century coaching inn. There are plenty of rocks on the surrounding hillsides, and the present owners intend building an ornamental fountain in the courtyard, so that the pub can live up to its name. This is the least of the many alterations and renovations planned for this group of buildings, and the seventeenth-century tithe barn on the hill above has already been converted into a grand banqueting hall. The pub itself is a tall, whitewashed building, with irregularly spaced windows (one with its original wooden frame) and capped by diagonal chimney stacks. It dates from the early seventeenth century, but archaeologists have identified several phases of work, as the original small house was extended and rebuilt over the years. In 1869 the inn closed and reverted to what was probably its original role, a farmhouse, but just over a hundred years later the buildings had become derelict and unsafe. Then in the 1970s a film producer purchased the Penhow estate and began a lengthy series of restoration work on the various buildings, principally the castle. For a time the inn was known as The Castle Arms and formed part of the Penhow heritage centre and film studio. Though no longer part of the property, it still caters for visitors to the nearby castle and for travellers who prefer the scenic A48 to the M4.

The interior has been thoroughly restored, and many rooms look completely modern (security cameras are an incongruous and unwelcome addition), but all the public areas of the inn are contained within the thick seventeenth-century walls, with most of the old ceiling beams intact. A restored inglenook adorns one end of the lounge, and in a wall-recess is a collection of pipe-makers' moulds and nineteenth-century carpenters' tools. The residents' lounge and guest room on the first floor retain their beamed ceilings, and a narrow stair leads up to the attic rooms, now light and comfortable, but once the dark and cheerless chambers of the servants and house staff.

Penhow lies on the A48 road between Chepstow (M4 junction 22) and Newport (junction 24). Bar snacks and meals, accommodation. Open 11 a.m.–3 p.m., 7–11 p.m.

The Six Bells, PETERSTONE WENTLOOGE
(ST 268 801)

Anyone from Norfolk may well feel at home on the Wentlooge levels, an area of low-lying coastal land drained by innumerable ditches (reens), with a few scattered villages and tall towered churches. The land here lies virtually at sea level, and only the great wharf holds back the tide. Land reclamation has been going on for centuries, and it was the Romans who first constructed dykes and cut ditches to drain the marshes. Nature, however, has a way of retaliating against Man's seeming victories, and in several of the local churches there are commemorative plaques which record the great flood of 1606. 'The foresaid waters having gotten over their wonted limittes, are affirmed to have runne at their first entrance with a swiftness so incredible, as that no grayhound could have escaped by running before them.' According to the same contemporary report, twenty-five towns and villages were 'all spoiled by the greevous and lamentable furie of the waters'.

The story of the flood, the history and archaeology of the Gwent levels, is outlined on a wall chart within the Six Bells at Peterstone. The name is said to derive from the six bells hung in the tower of the adjacent parish church, though Victorian restoration upped that number to eight. Small brass copies of the eponymous instruments hang above the bar, overlooked by a huge bristling boar's head. Photographs and drawings on the walls show the pub as it appeared in the early part of this century, before extensive refurbishment was carried out in the 1950s and '60s. The long and rather low building had small windows and a thatched roof; now slate replaces thatch, the roof has been heightened, and some windows enlarged. The bar retains an unusually broad fireplace and stone winding stair (which now no longer reaches the first floor since the ceiling was raised!).

There is a tradition that this seventeenth-century pub was once used as a brewery by the local clergy, and in more recent times it functioned as an almshouse, when it was split into five small cottages. The partitions survived until the 1960s when most were removed and the whole of the building restored for use by the drinking public.

The village of Peterstone lies on the Wentlooge levels between Newport and Cardiff. From M4 junction 28 at Tredegar follow the A48 to Newport, and at the first roundabout take the third turning off to St Brides Wentlooge. Follow this road (the B4239) for about 4 miles until you reach the village. The road continues on to Cardiff via Rumney. Bar snacks and meals. Open 11.30 a.m.–3 p.m., 7–11 p.m.

The Angel Inn, PONT NEDD FECHAN

(SN 900 077)

The Angel Inn stands guard at the mouth of a dark, wooded ravine, which winds its way upstream to some of the most spectacular waterfalls in Wales. Just beyond the pub car-park a narrow footpath heads into the gorge, past deep pools and rapids, overhanging cliffs, disused mines and mills, and finally ends at the cascade of Sgwd Gwladys – the Lady Falls. This is also known as the Angel Falls, though whether it was named after the pub or vice-versa is not known. Similar walks along the neighbouring Pyrddin and Mellte rivers will bring the tireless rambler to more geological wonders, all of which strengthen the district's almost official (and unrivalled) 'Waterfall Country' title.

The Angel was once a farmhouse, as a group of venerable looking outbuildings across the road indicates. Some have been sympathetically converted into a youth hostel and tourist information centre, where visitors can obtain details of all the walks and places of interest in this area of the Brecon Beacons National Park.

From the front the inn looks lop-sided, since the main bar and lounge catch the attention first, but its diminutive companion – a little cottage hanging on to the end – is the original part. The interior of this eighteenth-century lobby-entry house is much cosier and more homely than the adjoining lounge, and has an exposed stone fireplace and beamed ceiling. Old photographs on the wall show the inn as it appeared in the last century, when this district was still remote, and frequented only by those hardy travellers drawn to the natural wonders of the region.

The pub lies in the Vale of Neath, off the A465 Neath to Merthyr Tydfil road. At Glyn-neath village a signposted road leads to Pont Nedd Fechan. Bar meals. Open 11 a.m.–4 p.m., 6–11 p.m.; Sunday: 12–3 p.m.; 7–10.30 p.m.

The Horse and Jockey, PONTYMOEL

(SO 302 011)

Reputed to be 475 years old (and looking every day of it) the Horse and Jockey is a long, low, thatched building standing opposite the church of St Michael. Although there is no apparent evidence for such a precise date, the building may well date from the seventeenth century, with later additions more than doubling the original accommodation. According to tradition the inn was a frequent port of call for the tired and thirsty workmen heading home after a hard day's work at the Pontypool ironworks. The forges and blast furnaces were established here by Richard Hanbury in the reign of Queen Elizabeth, and there is an exhibition on the industrial heritage of the area in the canal-side toll cottage near the town centre. Over the years the interior of the inn has undergone considerable alterations, and part of the rear wall has been swept away for a bar and lounge extension. The oldest part of the Horse and Jockey is the upper lounge, with its low beamed ceiling and modest inglenook. A blocked opening beside the fireplace is probably the old entrance to a winding stair. Most of the existing windows are not original as the brick jambs reveal, and customers with time to spare can examine the bare stonework and see the outlines of the earlier blocked openings. The entrance has been moved around a bit too; the existing door is entirely modern, as old photographs of the inn show. The juke-box conceals one early doorway, and the outlines of another can be seen a few feet along the wall.

One lost relic of the inn (fortunately recorded and drawn by Fred Hando) is a painted ceramic jug 2$\frac{1}{2}$ ft high, made in 1837, and which could hold 13$\frac{1}{2}$ gallons. Accompanying this monster was a glass 'tot', which could hold up to 5 pints. It was the custom at Christmas-time for the tot to be filled with ale, and a sovereign offered to anyone who could down it in one. Male pride took a serious blow one year when a lady won the prize!

The inn lies just off the A4042 Newport to Abergavenny road, 1 mile east of Pontypool town centre, M4 junction 26. Bar meals. Open 12–3 p.m., 6–11 p.m.

The New Inn, PWLLMEYRIC
(ST 515 922)

When Viscount Torrington visited Wales in the summer of 1787, his memories of the country were far from rosy, and on several occasions he had the misfortune of staying at inns which failed to live up to his expectations. An entry in his travelogue records an attempted excursion from Chepstow: 'but e'er I had gone three miles, a violent shower drove me into a small public house, the New Inn at Poulmick for shelter'. He then churned out a diatribe against his lodgings at Chepstow, and from this we may assume that the New Inn proved acceptable to the fastidious gent.

This was a popular stopping place when the road alongside formed the main coastal route from England into Wales; now the M4 has taken over that task. In architectural terms the New Inn is a close cousin of the better-known Skirrid Inn (p. 42), since both were built within a few years of each other to an almost identical plan. From outside you can see the outlines of a blocked Tudor-arch doorway, which was once the main entrance and opened on to a central passage separating the hall and parlour rooms. The passage led straight through to the rear stair turret, giving maximum privacy and effective circulation to the occupants. The partitions on either side of the passage have been taken down, and the rooms thrown into one long bar-lounge with grand fireplaces at either end. According to legend the inn was built as a hostelry for pilgrims, by the bishops of Llandaff, who owned land here. Yet again there is nothing to suggest that the existing inn is older than 1600, though the story is not all that improbable as the medieval palace of the bishops stands only a short distance away at Mathern.

The New Inn stands beside the A48 Chepstow to Newport road, about 2 miles from M4 junction 22. Bar snacks and meals. Open 12–11 p.m.; Sunday: 12–3 p.m., 7.30–10.30 p.m.

The Ship Inn, RAGLAN
(SO 413 077)

From a window in the Great Hall at Raglan Castle the Marquis of Worcester sadly watched Cromwell's troops marching in through the gate to carry out their orders of pillage and destruction. Throughout the summer of 1646 this Royalist stronghold withstood the pounding of Roundhead cannon fire, but with the build-up of enemy firepower the Marquis realized that further resistance was useless, and decided to surrender. The order was passed to 'slight' the defences to prevent any future use, and gangs of workmen began dismantling the battlements and breaking down walls. This was a fate shared by many of the old castles recalled for service in the Civil War, but the loss was far greater at Raglan, more a stately home than a medieval fortress. The great library was pillaged, the fittings stripped, the formal garden dug up, and the extensive fishponds drained in search of treasure. When the demolition gangs had left, stone robbers and pilferers helped reduce the castle's splendour to stony ruin.

According to tradition, the landlord of the village inn was among the locals who decided to take advantage of this sudden abundance of good building

Raglan, the Ship Inn: cutaway reconstruction *c.* 1650. The central fireplace is said to have been brought from Raglan Castle

stone, and carted away a fireplace to be rebuilt in his tavern. Today, some three and a half centuries later, this stone fireplace is the main feature in the lounge of the Ship Inn. But, like so many of the stories concerning the origins of pubs, can this be true? Certainly the sides of the fireplace look roughly cut, as if it has been hacked to fit an existing opening, and the carvings on the jambs are of an earlier type than found elsewhere at the inn. The lintel has also been damaged, perhaps during its removal or as a result of Roundhead cannonfire?

Apart from the stone inglenook another feature to look out for is the original timber door-frame to the bar. The actual door may be that now used in the cellar, which has a finger latch and a massive wooden lock. The adjoining dining room was probably once the kitchen, since there is a brick bake-oven at the back of the fireplace. Upstairs the rooms are little altered, with half-timbered partitions, and in the attic four massive trusses, festooned with cobwebs, hold up the roof. The main bar and dining room are the oldest parts of the inn, dating probably from the first half of the seventeenth century; a second wing, which now houses another bar, was added a generation or two later.

Further alterations greatly enlarged the accommodation, and it is said that the adjoining shop was at one time incorporated into the premises. This must surely have been one of the largest inns in the county, and there were broad arched entrances for coaches to be driven through the building to the rear yard and stables. In fact one of these passageways was knocked through the middle of the kitchen, and exposed stonework of the interior walls bears the scars of that drastic alteration. On the attractive cobbled forecourt is a modern brick well covering one of the original water supplies for the village. It is now sealed off, but the present landlord intends to restore the well and reconnect the water supply. So perhaps in the near future Raglan spring water will find a place on the shelves next to the Perrier.

The village and castle of Raglan are situated beside the A40 and A449 roads, mid-way between Usk and Monmouth, M4 junction 24. Bar snacks and meals. Open 11.30 a.m.–3.30 p.m., 5.30–11 p.m.

The Bush Inn, ST HILARY
(ST 016 734)

It is almost to be expected that such a photogenic hamlet as St Hilary should have the accolade of 'Best kept village in Wales', as a signpost on the green proclaims. The main road has left St Hilary to itself, and hedged lanes draw the traveller off the busy Cowbridge road and into this rural community. As usual, it is the church which first catches the attention; and a fine specimen it is, with twelfth-century nave and chancel, fourteenth-century aisle, and an imposing sixteenth-century tower. Within there is a stone effigy of Sir Thomas Basset (d. 1423), lord of nearby Beaupre Castle.

In the shadow of the tower stands the Bush Inn, one of the oldest thatched

St Hilary, the Bush Inn: a straight joint in the masonry beside the bay window marks the extent of the original sixteenth-century house

houses in the village, and one of the least changed. It was built over 400 years ago in the closing years of the reign of Henry VIII, or during the brief rule of his son, Edward VI. At about the same time, the wealthy Bassets were rebuilding their 'castle' in the more fashionable Renaissance style. After calling at the Bush, visitors should drive the short distance to Beaupre to see the great complex of buildings there. The contrast could not be greater; but the Bush Inn is still lived in, while the Bassets' grand mansion is now an echoing shell.

Enter the lounge of the Bush and you enter another age. The bar itself and the electric lights are the only anachronistic intrusions. The great fireplace recess is still warmed by a log fire, and its massive timber lintel is boldly projected forwards on oak brackets. The heavy beamed ceiling and flagstone floor further add to the atmosphere of unaltered years. Half of the bar is housed in what was an outer room and entrance passage to the sixteenth-century hall, while more recent additions at either end of the building contain a lounge and a restaurant. The cuisine at the Bush has an Egon Ronay recommendation, and the varied menu offers temptations few can resist.

Finding a good meal is no longer a problem for Ianto Ffrank, the inn's resident phantom. He was once a highwayman who preyed on travellers crossing the windswept heights of Stalling Down on the road to Cowbridge. When not busy divesting hapless coach passengers of their valuables, Ianto was downing flagons at the Bush and, it seems, he was better at the latter than the former. The ineffective highwayman was made into a scapegoat by other thieves, and his final exploit at sheep stealing ended with his headlong flight from the authorities, past the inn and into the tangled woods below the village. Ianto was found hiding in a cave, and was taken to Pant y Lladron (thieves' hollow) on Stalling Down, and there hung on a gallows. His last feeble observation was that his demise would accomplish nothing, since there would be many more Ianto Ffranks to follow. More tangible than his shade is Ianto's cave-hideout in the woods which, unlike many similar caverns and secret passages in folk-tales, actually exists. In fact the 'cave' is one of the few visible reminders of a surprisingly large mining industry which existed in this rural setting around 1760. The green hilltop west of the village is scarred and pitted with disused shafts, and Ianto's cave is one of the tunnels driven through the rock in search of lead, galena and silver in the days before the Industrial Revolution.

St Hilary lies about 2 miles east of Cowbridge, off the A48 Cardiff road. Bar snacks and meals. Open 11 a.m.–11 p.m.

The Traveller's Rest, THORNHILL
(ST 158 843)

The Traveller's Rest is a border pub in more ways than one. It stands like a half-way house on a mountain top which marks the start of the Glamorgan uplands, and were it not for the encroaching woodland there would be a splendid view from here over the Bristol Channel to Somerset and Avon. The Rest also marks the former boundary between the Welsh-ruled hill country, and the more fertile low-lying lands wrested from them by the Normans. The native prince of this region started to build a castle on the summit, but the Normans got there first! Now the forgotten walls crumble away in the woods behind the pub.

At night the pub is a thatched beacon aglow with coloured lights, a welcoming haven inviting in the traveller on the lonely mountain road between Cardiff and Caerphilly. Even in the more objective light of day, the pub embodies a 'picture postcard' atmosphere – look at the tiny first-floor windows barely peering from beneath the eaves, the stumpy chimneys struggling to rise above the shaggy thatch, and the thick walls constructed from huge rounded boulders. Inside the picture is even more remarkable, with knobbly stonework, a deep and very sooty inglenook, and blackened beams so low that any tall customer will scrape the ceiling. The bar is now housed in the original part of this eighteenth-century cottage, while the lounge and restaurant occupy a later wing at one end (with better headroom!).

The Traveller's Rest lies alongside the A469 road from Cardiff centre to Caerphilly, M4 junction 32. Bar snacks and meals. Open 11.30 a.m.–3 p.m., 6–11 p.m.

The Cross Keys, USK
(SO 375 008)

Along with its neighbours on the same river, Caerleon and Abergavenny, the town of Usk was founded by the Romans over nineteen centuries ago. Nero's fort lasted only a few years before it was replaced by Caerleon, and it was up to the Normans to stamp their mark on the future landscape and topography of the town. Modern progress has barely affected Usk, and the medieval street layout remains unchanged. At the east edge of the town stands the austere priory church, while from the wooded hilltop the overgrown castle stands guard over the houses clustered below. When the army of Owain Glyndwr attacked Usk in 1405 the town was razed but the castle held out, and the English garrison mercilessly routed the Welsh force. Economic recovery was slow, and as late as 1799 Archdeacon Coxe could write: 'many ancient houses are in ruins, and a considerable district is much dilapidated'. A map of Usk accompanying that description in his *Historical tour in Monmouthshire* bears little resemblance to the town today. Only a few buildings are shown standing alongside the old streets, and where there were once houses stretch open fields and pastures. In 1731 another traveller had passed through the district, and wrote: 'the situation is good, the Town neat, only the houses being built out of a coarse stone, the walls are thick, and the rooms dark. But this is the general way of the country, unless they build with timber or plaster'. Coxe, too, noted that 'several of the houses are faced with hewn stone, and from the form of the windows seem to have been constructed at an early period'. It would appear that there were more medieval buildings standing then, or perhaps the locals had plundered carved stones from the castle and priory buildings for use in their own homes.

Beside the road to Usk bridge stands the Cross Keys Inn, the oldest of the town pubs and arguably the most photogenic. The bowed walls of the building and low slate roof (once thatched) give a good indication of age, as do the stumpy chimneys, though the central one has gone. In spring and summer the plain whitewashed walls are brightened up by hanging baskets and tubs brimming with flowers. The large mounting block at one corner recalls the long-gone days when the only form of overland transport was a horse. Just inside the front door is a brass plaque and photographs which record two disastrous floods, in 1960 and 1979, when the Usk inundated the street to a depth of over 4 ft. There are now two main rooms, a lounge and dining area, and the bar between them occupies the site of a fireplace.

At the back of the dining room a passage leads to a low cellar reached by a flight of stone steps, and lit only by a tiny barred window. Such a curious

Usk, the Cross Keys

feature has inevitably led to the suggestion that this was once a prison. Although this seems unlikely the cellar and dining room appear to be older than the rest of the inn, and could be the remains of a late medieval building which was adapted and incorporated into the inn around 1600. The lounge has an impressive inglenook with an arched doorway on one side leading to the stair, and on the other a recess which marks the position of the original entrance. Over the plain lintel of the fireplace a carved oak mantelpiece has been affixed. This fine piece of craftsmanship was clearly meant to grace an ornamental fireplace elsewhere in the house – or did it in fact come from another building? One of the private rooms on the first floor has a decorated plaster ceiling, similar to that in the White Hart at Llangybi (p. 46). A second winding stair leads up to the attic chambers.

In November 1958 the Cross Keys was the scene of a remarkable attempt by reporters and spiritualists to unravel the mystery of a haunted room on the first floor. The new landlord, Mr Hoffman, was much puzzled by the behaviour of the bedroom door: 'No matter how firmly the latch is fastened, it still manages to raise itself,' he reported to the local newspaper. A week later, a group of reporters decided to go ghost hunting with cameras and tape recorders, and stayed overnight in the room. Hour after sleepy hour they waited for something unusual to happen, the only light in the room provided by a flickering candle. Then, at 5 a.m., the door slowly opened and a cold draught blew out the flame. The candle was again lit and the door shut, but after a while the same thing happened. This event was enough to provoke a group of spiritualists from Blackwood to hold a seance in the room, and while in a trance a medium succeeded in communicating with the restless spirit. The ghost was that of a seventeenth-century foreign girl, named Clare or Clara Bernhardt, who poisoned herself when she was imprisoned in this room by her guardians. An unapproved love affair seems to have been the cause of the trouble, and a later elaboration of the story claims that Clara ended her life by eating ivy leaves and berries. The medium pleaded with the spirit to stop seeking a physical way out of the room by opening the door, but instead to 'pass into the light'. The group finally left the inn, confident that they had laid the 300-year-old ghost to rest – but the door still opens!

Usk lies just off the A449 Newport to Monmouth road, on the A472 to Pontypool. Bar snacks and meals. Open 11.30 a.m.–3 p.m., 6.30–11 p.m.

Additional inns and taverns

Aberdulais, Dulais Rock (SS 771 993)
Abergavenny, Coach and Horses (SO 300 140)
Aberthin, Fox and Hounds (ST 008 753)
Caerphilly, Court House (ST 156 868)
Kenfig, Prince of Wales (SS 804 817)
Llancarfan, Fox and Hounds (ST 052 703)
Llanhamlach, Old Ford Inn (SO 092 262)
Llanishen, Church Inn (ST 176 817)
Llanharry, Bear Inn (ST 006 805)
Llanthony, Priory Hotel (SO 288 278)
Llantilio Crossenny, Hostrey (SO 396 146)
Llysworney, Carne Arms (SS 964 740)
Pentyrch, King's Arms (ST 104 818)
Rhoose, Fontygary Inn (ST 051 663)
Rudry, Maenllwyd Inn (ST 201 866)
St George's, Greendown Inn (ST 105 765)
Skenfrith, Bell Inn (SO 457 202)
Tretower, Nantyffin Cider Mill (SO 197 199)
Tintern, Royal George Hotel (SO 530 001)
Wick, Lamb and Flag (SS 924 722)

3. THE SOUTHERN MARCHES

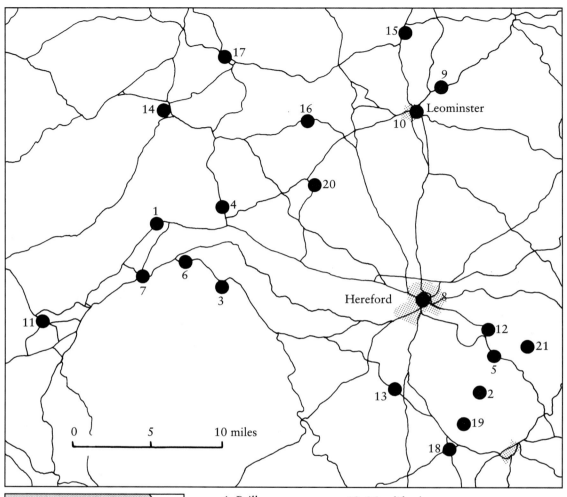

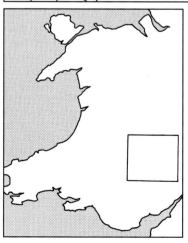

1. Brilley
2. Carey
3. Dorstone
4. Eardisley
5. Fownhope
6. Hardwick
7. Hay-on-Wye
8. Hereford
9. Kimbolton
10. Leominster
11. Llyswen

12. Mordiford
13. Much Dewchurch
14. Old Radnor
15. Orleton
16. Pembridge
17. Presteigne
18. St Owen's Cross
19. Sellack
20. Weobley
21. Woolhope

The Rhydspence Inn, BRILLEY
(SO 244 473)

For hundreds of years the Rhydspence Inn was a major port of call for the Welsh drovers leading their herds along the Wye valley to the markets at Hereford. Not only did the sixteenth-century inn offer refreshment and accommodation (at least to those who could afford it), but it also marked the border between England and Wales, at a point where the river was shallow enough to be forded. Alongside the inn stood a smithy, where the cattle would be shod for the next stage of the trek.

Although claimed to date from the fourteenth century, the main part of the inn was built in the sixteenth century, and the close-set timber framing is a typical feature of the age. From the large and pleasant gardens at the rear, customers can see the change in timberwork and the masonry walls which indicates that the inn was extended, or rebuilt, in later centuries. At least these alterations blend in with the older parts less obtrusively than the modern three-storey hotel wing at one end; an unfortunate testimony to the popularity of the inn. Nevertheless there is consolation to be gained from the public areas of the Rhydspence, with its half-timbered partitions, beamed ceilings and grand stone fireplace. The building is entered through a tipsy porch supported on carved posts, with the dining room on the left, and the twin bar-lounges to the right.

According to tradition the inn straddles the border and there used to be a rumpus on Sundays when the Radnorshire half was dry, and the Herefordshire half wet! But in fact the actual border line is the insignificant brook which trickles through the garden, and there used to be two inns here, which probably gave rise to the story. At midnight on May Day 1873, the diarist Francis Kilvert walked through Rhydspence, and found the English inn 'still ablaze with light and noisy with the songs of revellers, but the Welsh inn was dark and still'. Obviously the natives of this area respected the licensing laws – or maybe they were over the border enjoying a late pint?

The Rhydspence occupies a prominent location beside the A438 Hereford to Hay-on-Wye road, about 3 miles from Hay. Bar snacks and meals, accommodation. Open 11 a.m.–2.30 p.m., 7–11 p.m.; Sunday: 12–2 p.m., 7–11 p.m.

The Cottage of Content, CAREY
(SO 563 310)

On the banks of the Wye beyond the remarkable Italianate church of Hoarwithy stands the village of Carey and the aptly named Cottage of Content. A little stream wanders past the pub, where it is crossed by a humpbacked bridge far larger than needed for such a watery obstacle. In spring and summer the outside of the pub is a mass of vibrant colour, with the gardens and hanging baskets overflowing with flowers. Before the fortuitous name-change put Carey on the map, the pub was prosaically known as the Miners' Arms, and local residents still remember when the building was divided into three workmen's cottages. Originally this was a single dwelling dating from the seventeenth century; much of the interior has changed little over the years, although some partition walls have come down, and the large back-to-back fireplaces have been modernized. The picnic benches on the steep hillside behind offer a good vantage point from which to view the inn, and from this side the original appearance of the half-timbered building can be appreciated. Most of the other walls have been rebuilt in brick and stone. Inside there are three lounges with flagstone floors and beamed ceilings, and the central room preserves an original unglazed window – a reminder of the time when glass was a luxury item available only to those with enough money in their pockets.

From Hereford follow the B4399 to Holme Lacy until, just before the village, a right fork leads to Bolstone and on to Carey. Alternatively, from the A49 Ross-on-Wye road follow the signposted minor roads to Hoarwithy. Just past the church a signposted turning leads along the riverside for 1¹/₂ miles to Carey. Bar meals, accommodation. Open 12–2.30 p.m., 7–11 p.m.

The Pandy Inn, DORSTONE
(SO 313 417)

When Henry II uttered those infamous words 'who will rid me of this turbulent priest?' he set in motion a train of events which led, ultimately, to the building of an inn on the Welsh Marches. Four knights mistook Angevin wrath for a royal command, and galloped off to carry out the barbarous act. Archbishop Thomas à Becket, Henry's one-time friend and confidant, was hacked to death on the steps of the altar in his cathedral at Canterbury. The *coup de grâce* was delivered by one Richard de Brito, the force of the blow causing his sword to break in two on the bloodstained floor. Society was aghast at the crime. Despite Henry's protestations of innocence, he was criticized by the Pope and forced to do public penance. As for the murderers they were banished overseas to do military service with the Knights Templar, a band of warrior monks sworn to defend the Holy Sepulchre at Jerusalem, and protect pilgrims visiting the Christian shrines.

Richard de Brito spent some fifteen years in the Holy Land before returning to England and settling in Golden Valley in West Herefordshire. There he set about rebuilding the parish church of Dorstone, to expiate his lingering guilt, or at least prove to the locals that he was a reformed man. The craftsmen employed to do the work were housed in a newly built tavern across the market-place from the church. This, according to popular legend, is the origin

Dorstone, Pandy Inn: cutaway view of this seventeenth-century hearth-passage house

of the Pandy Inn, but like so many of the tales told about other 'ancient' inns there is no real evidence to show that the existing building is as old as the legend suggests. Part of the tale may be true, for when the church was rebuilt again, in 1889, an inscribed stone was discovered which recorded the founding of a chapel here by one John de Brito in 1256. He is said to have been Richard's nephew, although it has been pointed out that Brito ('the Breton') was a common surname in medieval England, and that Beckett's killer had ties with Somerset rather than the Welsh border. But let us leave such tales alone, while they are still modestly attired in semi-historical garb.

The inn itself almost certainly dates from the seventeenth century, and it is a good example of a hearth passage house; the original 'front door' was beside the massive projecting chimney (as shown in the reconstruction drawing). Customers now enter via another door knocked through the side wall, and this is the least obvious of the many alterations the original building has been subjected to. Later in the seventeenth, or sometime in the eighteenth century, an additional wing was built at the rear resulting in an L-shaped plan. This now houses a lounge and games room. Most of the ground-floor partitions have recently been altered and so it is not clear how the rooms were arranged originally, but the large gable inglenook in the bar would certainly have warmed the hall. In contrast the first floor is little changed, although these rooms are not, of course, accessible to the public. There are original doors, exposed timber framing and an open roof, all lovingly restored. What is particularly interesting about this pub is that, lying so close to mountainous Wales, it has the external appearance of a typical stone-built hill farm, but the interior is entirely half-timbered and characteristic of the 'black and white' houses a few miles further east.

The name of the inn derives from the adjacent *pandy*, or fulling mill, behind which stand the earthworks of a motte and bailey castle. The stream which powered the millwheel also separates the village from the church, and is one of many rivulets draining the ridges on either side of the valley. To the ancient Celts this was the 'vale of water' -*Dur*, or *Dwr* in modern Welsh, a name the invading Normans chose to reinterpret as *D'or*, gold. The Celts were no doubt nearer the mark, since geologists believe that the marshy valley bottom north of the village is the site of a lake left by a glacier thousands of years ago. The only gold to be found in the valley today is the acres of ripening summer corn and barley. The nineteenth-century cleric and diarist Francis Kilvert wrote how he climbed the hill above the village, and had 'a glorious view of the Golden Valley shining in the evening sunlight, with the white houses of Dorstone scattered about the green hillsides "like a handful of pearls in a cup of emerald"'. It is a peaceful image with which to leave Golden Valley, paying little attention to the numerous castles dotted around, which hint that tranquillity did not always reign here.

The village lies in Golden Valley between Hay-on-Wye and Pontrilas, off the B4348. Bar meals. Open 12–3 p.m., 7–11 p.m. Closed Monday and Tuesday lunchtimes in winter.

The Tram Inn, EARDISLEY
(SO 312 492)

Eardisley is another Herefordshire 'picture postcard' village of half-timbered houses, but here, closer to the Welsh mountains, stone makes more of an appearance. At one end of the single street stands the tall towered parish church, containing a richly decorated Norman font, which reveals that the builders of so many grim and forbidding castles were imbued with a piously aesthetic streak. Beyond the churchyard an insignificant overgrown earthwork is all that remains of an eleventh-century castle, although this may be a misnomer, since it is listed in the Domesday book as a '*Domus defensibilis*', or fortified house.

From the church the narrow street wanders northwards, past magpie buildings lined up for inspection, and where the road widens and forks there stands the Tram Inn. Even a cursory glance at the exterior reveals a building of more than one period, with different size timbers and varying framing patterns highlighting the changes. Just beside the modern porch can be seen the outlines of a blocked Tudor-arch door, which originally led into the cross-passage separating the hall from lesser service rooms. This plan is repeated in many medieval and sixteenth-century houses along the Marches, and can be traced in the Black Swan (p. 96), the Pembridge Inn (p. 101) and the Butcher's Arms (p. 109). At the Tram, however, internal renovations carried out in the seventeenth century have almost totally obscured the original plan. High up in the dusty, cobwebbed attic is a single carved roof truss, grimed with centuries of soot from an open hearth, a sure indication that this inn was once a late medieval open hall. The reconstruction drawing gives some indication of the noble proportions of the original hall, before the insertion of floors and ceilings.

For railway buffs there is a leaflet available at the bar outlining the history of the Eardisley tramway, which was built between 1812 and 1818 and ran through Hay to Brecon. Welsh coal was brought one way, and lime and corn the other. The sturdy horses which dragged the trams across country were

Eardisley, the Tram Inn: cutaway reconstruction of the timber-framed hall, *c.* 1500. Most of the details shown still survive, although the position of some of the windows is conjectural, and it is assumed that there were additional rooms beyond the hall (shown right) which no longer exist

stabled at the inn, while their equally exhausted drivers slaked their thirst inside. The primitive tramway has long gone, but a piece of the metal track is on display in the lounge. When the Eardisley estate was sold off in 1918 the landlady of the Tram, Ellen Baird, bought the inn for the princely sum of £1,100. An old photograph on the lounge wall shows the outside of the inn earlier this century, with a newfangled motor car parked on the forecourt. Standing alongside is a lady in black, who is thought to be Mrs Baird. She has been seen at the Tram long after her death, and so whisky is not the only spirit you could find here.

Eardisley lies on the A4111 Willersley to Kington road, about 2 miles off the main A438 between Hereford and Brecon. Bar snacks and meals. Open 12–2.30 p.m., 6–11 p.m.

The Green Man Inn, FOWNHOPE
(SO 577 345)

The leaf-wreathed face of the Green Man is perhaps the oldest image which has survived from our pagan past. And yet it may come as a surprise to realize that the place where the Green Man is most often found is a church or cathedral. What caused the medieval masons and carpenters to re-create the verdant visage inside the holiest of places? Did the concept of a man fully integrated with nature appeal to them, or was it the symbolism of the regenerative and fertile land translated into the religious ideals of life after death? The Norman church at Kilpeck a few miles away has its Green Man, as well as a notorious female fertility symbol. The inn at Fownhope is the oldest pub in Wales and the Marches to bear this name, and the sign depicts a group of maypole dancers and a crowned figure dressed in leaves. This is Jack-in-the-green, a more recent incarnation of the Green Man, who plays an important role in May Day festivities around the country. Even the overly familiar Robin Hood may be just another aspect of the woodland spirit.

As originally built the inn consisted of two timber-framed buildings at right angles, the main hall facing the road, with a kitchen wing at the rear. Documents mention an inn here in 1485 called the Naked Boy, but the existing building contains no details earlier than 1600. Most of the inn was here when the Roundhead leader, Colonel Birch, stopped by on his way to

Fownhope, the Green Man Inn

Hereford, during the siege of Goodrich Castle in 1645. The original building has been considerably extended since then, and the later work can be detected by the liberal use of brick and false timber-framing. The interior has also been restored and enlarged beyond the seventeenth-century wings, so that there are now several large rooms opening off each other at different levels.

The Judge's Bar was probably the old kitchen and has an impressive inglenook; the name recalls the time when the inn was used as a petty court, and on the wall is a framed pamphlet of 1820 which lists the allowances granted to policemen transporting vagrants and criminals to prison. Next door the 'Tom Spring' bar commemorates Fownhope's most famous son, Thomas Winter, a bare-fist fighter and heavyweight champion of England, born here in 1795. In those days the inn was a frequent stopping place for travellers on the old road (now the B4224) between Hereford and Gloucester, and the coaching yard and stables where their horses were kept still remains. All the buildings around the yard have been modernized and turned into guest accommodation, but fortunately the old sign over the entrance has been left to act as an advertisement for present-day travellers: 'You travel far, You travel near, its here you find the best of beer. You pass the East, You pass the West, if you pass this you pass the Best.' Anyone coming in from the west also had to pass the village stocks beside the churchyard, a sobering reminder of what was in store for drunken troublemakers!

Fownhope village lies in the Wye valley about 4 miles south-east of Hereford, on the B4224 to Ross-on-Wye. Bar snacks and meals, accommodation. Open 11 a.m.–2.30 p.m., 6–11 p.m.

The Royal Oak, HARDWICKE
(SO 273 437)

On a gentle hilltop above the valley of the winding Wye stands this long, low and whitewashed seventeenth-century building. Like so many of the houses built close to the Welsh mountains the exterior walls are thick stone, while all the interior partitions are half-timbered. Look closely at the upright posts and you can trace a series of esoteric carpenter's marks, which enabled the builder to correctly assemble the prefabricated timbers. A step up through a carved timber door leads to the lounge and dining area, which is said to have been converted from a cowshed when the inn was a farmhouse.

The name of the pub greets you on the doorstep in ceramic tiles, and much of the interior is floored with decorative tiles which once graced a local church. The 'Royal Oak' refers to the story of the fugitive Charles II hiding in a tree to escape his pursuers, but Hardwicke has a better claim to this than most pubs. Thomas Whitney, lord of the surrounding district of Clifford, was a friend of the exiled monarch during the Commonwealth, and on the king's return in 1660 Thomas was enrolled into the newly founded 'Knights of the Royal Oak' in recognition of his support.

The furniture too has a story to tell. In the bar there is an old wooden settle with a chest beneath the seat, and in this, so we are told, poachers would hide their spoils should the bailiff appear. One elderly local remembers an event in his childhood when he was hastily concealed in the chest by his father, who spied the approach of a policeman. Much to the amusement of everyone present, the policeman then ordered a pint and sat down on the chest to drink it!

Hardwicke lies on the B4348 road to Dorstone, 2¹/₂ miles north-east of Hay-on-Wye. Bar snacks and meals, accommodation. Open 11 a.m.–3 p.m., 6–11 p.m.

HAY-ON-WYE

(SO 230 424)

Until the reorganization of 1974, the charming book town of Hay-on-Wye stood at the junction of three counties, Brecon, Radnor and Hereford, and its strategic border location meant it was in for a rough time. Founded by the Normans, the town and castle were frequent targets for Welsh animosity, and thanks to plague, war and declining trade, Hay was 'wonderfully decayed' by the sixteenth century, as John Leland observed. Following the Reformation there was a long, slow period of recovery and growth, and by the early nineteenth century the topographer Samuel Lewis could give a much more optimistic picture of the town: 'the streets in many places have been widened, and divers unsightly obstructions removed; old houses have been modernized, and new ones of a highly respectable character built including an excellent inn and posting house'. That would have been the Swan, still one of the main hostelries in the town. Hay preserves several of its old buildings, along with a tortuous street system, though Lewis's statements suggest that much has gone for good.

Apart from the imposing castle-cum-mansion, the oldest standing building in town is believed to be the Three Tuns, the 'first and last' pub in Wales, since it stands on the road leading over the river into England. This is very much a collector's item. Few other pubs in the country can claim to be so little changed in a hundred years. The Tuns is something of a throwback to the days when every town and village tavern was little more than the front room of someone's house, and where beer and ale was hand-drawn from casks and served in pitchers. The unmodernized and cluttered interior was used in the film *On the Black Hill*, a moving portrayal of a farming family living in the nearby Black Mountains. Lucy Powell, the present venerable landlady, has worked here all her life, and the Powells have held the Three Tuns for generations. Some 'sensitive' customers have claimed the pub is haunted, but I have it on good authority that the landlady has 'never heard a tinkle'. Both interior and exterior give little indication of the age of the building, for only a few old beams are visible, but this was originally a sixteenth-century timber-framed hall house. The hall was open to the rafters, and the roof supported on massive curving cruck trusses which rise from ground level. In a typical seventeenth-century modification, an upper floor was put into the hall, and the smoky open hearth replaced with a brick chimney. The present bar occupies a single room in a cross-wing at one end of the hall.

If, on the other hand, you prefer pubs to be thoroughly modernized, with plenty of bare stonework and blackened beams hung with horse-brasses, then the award-winning Old Black Lion is for you. Oliver Cromwell is said to have been a guest here, though since he was besieging the castle at the time he would hardly have been a popular visitor. Neither were the early Methodist ministers, and one William Seward (a friend of the great reformer Howell Harris) was struck by a stone and killed while remonstrating to a crowd outside the inn, in 1740. The Black Lion is said to date from the thirteenth century, though the visible details are seventeenth century, and much of the interior has been greatly altered. Some partitions have been taken down, others put up, old beams go this way and that, and rooms open off rooms. Altogether this is a pleasantly confusing building, with a superb guest room on the first floor with an open balcony – a perfect setting for a romantic weekend.

The town of Hay-on-Wye lies in the Wye valley between Brecon and Hereford, on the A438. Old Black Lion: Bar snacks and meals, accommodation. Open 11 a.m.–3 p.m., 6–11 p.m.

HEREFORD
(SO 510 400)

If the visitor to historic Hereford is understandably overwhelmed by the
glories of cathedral architecture, there is a wealth of secular monuments to
bring the gaze down from the heavens. Cromwell left little of the castle for us
to admire, but there are still many of the timber-framed buildings which were
standing when the Roundhead troops marched through the narrow streets.
Here and there the gleam of magpie houses draws the eye away from red
sandstone and grey concrete, and even those shops which outwardly look new
often have the skeletons of their timbered forebears encased within.

Hereford, the Black Lion

One such building is the Grapes Tavern, just off the delightful lane which links the main street to the cathedral precincts. In 1989 the derelict and dilapidated building was surveyed by the City of Hereford Archaeology Unit, and it became apparent that behind the nondescript Victorian exterior there was preserved an almost intact seventeenth-century house. After an extensive programe of renovation work the façade has been restored to its original appearance, with oversailing upper floors crowned by dormers. Unfortunately not enough remained of the timber panels and decorations to be reconstructed, but similar buildings surviving in the city give an idea of what the tavern once looked like.

Of the other city pubs the most outwardly impressive is the late sixteenth-century Black Lion in Bridge Street. Like the Grapes this originally had overhanging upper floors, but has been underbuilt in brick – an inevitable alteration carried out on such buildings when the jettied timbers begin to give way. Although the interior is less distinguished, there is an upper room containing a remarkable series of wall-paintings discovered in 1932. They depict the Ten Commandments and, like wall-paintings in certain churches, were designed to be understood by the literate few and illiterate masses. The panels show biblical characters (in Tudor costume) breaking each commandment, with an accompanying inscription providing further information for those who could read. 'Thou shalt doe noe Murder' screams the headline above the scene of Joab killing Amasa (Samuel 2). Other modernized seventeenth–century timber buildings include the Black Swan (Bewell Street), the Spread Eagle, with medieval cellars (Bewell Street) and the White Hart, which has a decorated plaster ceiling on the second floor (Broad Street).

Anyone wishing to know more about life and society in seventeenth-century Hereford should visit the 'Old House' museum in the market square. This tall, half-timbered building is the only survivor of an entire row, and has been restored and furnished in original style, giving an excellent impression of day-to-day life three centuries ago.

The city of Hereford lies in the Wye valley between Leominster and Ross-on-Wye. There are several good routes to follow, including the A49 from Ross, or the A417 from M50 junction 2. Bar meals. Open 11 a.m.–3 p.m., 6–11 p.m.

The Stockton Cross, KIMBOLTON
(SO 520 612)

Only an undulating meadow on the sloping banks of the Cogwell Brook marks the site of the medieval village of 'Stocktune' mentioned in the Domesday Book. Up above on the hilltop a glorious group of sixteenth- and seventeenth-century black-and-white cottages huddle around the crossroads. The main east to west route links Tenbury Wells to Leominster, while the lesser tracks fan out into the Herefordshire countryside. Strangely the bespired parish church stands on a hill half a mile away, so that the close association between church and pub (so obvious in many other villages) is hardly evident here. And the Stockton Cross looks more like a picture-postcard cottage than a pub; only the unobtrusive sign by the door gives the game away. The most impressive feature of this half-timbered seventeenth-century inn is the huge stone chimney at one end, with an equally imposing inglenook inside. Upright slabs support a thick oak lintel under which a log fire crackles in cold weather. The main bar is housed in the central room of this three-part house, although most of the timber-framed dividing walls have come down. The interior is now a long, low room, with various later additions including a quiet dining area half hidden behind the ponderous chimney.

The pub stands beside the A4112 to Tenbury Wells, just off the A49 2 miles north-east of Leominster.

LEOMINSTER
(SO 495 590)

Leominster's noble priory church rears up out of the bustle of medieval and modern houses clustered about the maze-like streets. Hidden away are a number of old pubs and inns which, for hundreds of years, served refreshments to the merchants of this historic market town.

There may well have been a Roman settlement here, but the place-name reveals that the town's origins lie in Anglo-Saxon times. Earl Leofric and his wife Godiva founded a nunnery here in the ninth century, and 'Leofric's minster' survived until the Reformation. There were a few problems along the way; in 1046 the Danish Earl Swein had his wicked way with the abbess, and the nunnery was closed down 'for its sins' – so perhaps the lady was not such an unwilling victim as we might suppose. Inside the medieval church is a remarkable eighteenth-century ducking stool, where nagging wives were dunked in the river – no doubt to the satisfaction of their husbands! A plaque also informs us that this punishment was meted out to 'butchers, bakers, brewers, apothecaries, and all else who give short measure'.

The most impressive of the early pubs is the Three Horseshoes, just off the market square. This corner building dates to *c.* 1600 and has a long, jettied upper floor leaning drunkenly over a narrow lane which runs alongside. To walk down this lane is to recapture something of the daily life in Tudor towns, with overhanging buildings crowding out the sky, and grabbing as much space out and up – since any sideways growth was inevitably hampered by neighbouring properties. The front façade would have been overhanging as well, but this side has been underbuilt in brick. Inside there are two spacious well-lit rooms, a bar and a lounge; but mortice holes in the beams show where partitions have been taken down, and so the interior would have been very much more cramped and dark generations ago. In fact, the pub was originally

Leominster, the Chequers Inn

two tenements built side by side, and although the party wall has been taken down there is still an abrupt drop in floor level. This is very much a young people's pub, though there is a nice collection of old prints in the lounge, and an unusual arrangement of horseshoes of various sizes mounted on the wall.

At the further end of the town centre, in Etnam Street, stands the Chequers Inn, which along with its neighbour forms an attractive group of half-timbered buildings. A little further down the road is the Lion, less obviously as old since the façade has been rendered, but at the back there is an impressive jettied upper floor running the whole length of the building. If the rendering were stripped away and the timbered panels exposed, then this sixteenth-century inn would be another jewel in Leominster's architectural crown.

Leominster is situated midway between Hereford and Ludlow on the A49. Three Horseshoes: Bar meals. Open 10.30 a.m.–11 p.m., Sunday: 12–3 p.m., 7–10 p.m.

The Griffin Inn, LLYSWEN
(SO 132 379)

Lying so close to the banks of the Wye, it is hardly surprising that a fishing theme dominates the interior decor of the Griffin Inn. For centuries the inhabitants of this inn and the surrounding cottages would have fished for salmon, though it is doubtful that fish as large as the one displayed in the lounge were caught often. This 33 lb specimen was landed below the village in 1986 and now adorns the wall beside the bar. A ginger tom was gazing wistfully at it on my visit.

The inn lies at the junction of the main Builth to Hay turnpike road, and it is clear that the road was here before the inn – since the lower lounge and dining room have been built off at an angle to avoid getting hit by vehicles negotiating the tight bend. But the oldest part of the Griffin is the central section which now houses the bar. There were once two fireplaces heating separate rooms, but later modifications have altered the interior layout and now only one inglenook remains, along with a few original ceiling beams. The inn is said to date from 1467, but like so many other claims there is no visible architectural evidence to support such an early origin. But the central bar-lounge is clearly earlier than the two adjoining rooms which appear to be late seventeenth- or eighteenth-century additions. One of these, the upper lounge, has a large restored inglenook with a brick bake-oven at the side, and was evidently the kitchen. There is little exposed stonework displaying joints and abutments to help date the various parts of the building, and in any case the whitewashed exterior is almost entirely shrouded in a thick wreath of foliage.

Llyswen was visited by Wordsworth and his sister in 1798, but a guidebook written a hundred years later warned that there was no accommodation fit for ladies at the village. This is no longer the case; and even the guest rooms at the Griffin are named after fishing flies.

The inn stands at the junction of the A4079 with the A470 road to Builth Wells, about 7 miles south-west of Hay-on-Wye. Bar snacks and meals, accommodation. Open 11 a.m.–3 p.m., 6–11 p.m., Winter: 12–2.30 p.m., 7–11 p.m.

The Moon Inn, MORDIFORD
(SO 572 374)

East of Hereford the B4224 road to Ross meanders along the Wye valley before skirting the wooded hills around Mordiford and Fownhope. Travellers in olden times had to endure more than the ever-present threat of cut-throats and highwaymen; the roads were often little more than muddy cattle tracks, and even minor rivers and streams proved a daunting (and damp) obstacle for anyone unable to afford a horse. According to some of the darker stories about Mordiford, getting wet was the least of the problems a wayfarer could suffer here. At least the traveller safely entering the village from the west could raise a thankful glance heavenward, while crossing the sturdy stone bridge to the hospitality of the local tavern. Apart from the Victorianized parish church, the Lugg bridge is the oldest relic in the village, being built in 1352 and still carrying traffic over the fast flowing river.

The Moon Inn was certainly not here when the bridge was built, although there was undoubtedly another tavern and hostel in the village. There are said to be accounts which record the construction of this half-timbered pub in 1603 at a cost of £17, and a further 19s 7d for internal woodwork and ironwork. It is likely that this building consisted of only the present bar area, for although some of the partitions have been removed, enough survives to indicate that the house had a typical plan comprising a hall and service rooms separated by a cross-passage. The hall fireplace is particularly impressive, with

Mordiford, the Moon Inn: the existing roofs are modern, and the line of the steeply pitched seventeenth-century roofs can be seen in the gable end

a thick, rugged timber lintel propped up by upright stone slabs. A kitchen wing (still used as such) was added at the rear a few years later, resulting in an L-shaped plan. This simple layout was further complicated when an entirely new block (now the bar-lounge) was built on the opposite side of the hall, probably towards the end of the seventeenth century. The much finer detailing on the woodwork and the heavy, cross-beamed ceiling hints that this room was the 'showpiece' of the house, and was probably used as a parlour. More unusual is the fact that the walls were constructed of local stone, rather than half-timbering.

For just under 390 years the Moon Inn has stood on its elevated site in the village, overlooking a little bridge which crosses the Pentaloe brook. It was surely this location that saved the pub from destruction in 1811, when a terrible storm 'of thunder, lightning, wind and rain' turned the insignificant stream into a raging torrent. The churning, muddy waters overflowed the banks and swept into the village, bearing with it an almost solid mass of boulders, rubble, trees and debris, which swept away buildings, damaged the church and killed four people.

Another, less factual, disaster to befall the normally quiet village was the onslaught of a dragon, which lurked in nearby Haugh Wood. According to the story, it was found as a 'baby' by a young girl who reared it as a pet, but soon it grew too large and fearsome and eventually escaped into the forest. From the seclusion of its leafy den the serpent would crawl down to drink at the Lugg, and then feast on anything not quick enough to run away. The villagers were all too frightened to slay the dragon, but a condemned criminal named Garson bravely took up the challenge, and hid himself in a barrel at the water's edge. As the great reptile slid past the innocuous-looking barrel, Garson fired a fatal arrow through the bung-hole. An alternative version of the tale exists, in which the criminal placed knives and barbs around the outside of the barrel, on which the dragon cut itself to pieces trying to get at its dinner inside. Whichever method was used it was a two-edged blow, since the poisonous breath of the dying reptile also finished off the would-be hero. Until the flood of 1811 when the church was drastically restored, a wall-painting of a green dragon could be seen at the west end of the building. Underneath was an inscription which read:

> This is the true effigy of the strange
> Prodigious monster, which our wood did range.
> In Eastwood it by Garson's Hand was slayne,
> A truth which old mythologists maintayne.

Whether this was painted in remembrance of some semi-historical event, or whether the story arose because of it, is not known. More level-headed observers have pointed out that the painted dragon could simply have been one of the heraldic beasts depicted on the arms of St Guthlac's priory in Hereford.

Mordiford village lies 2¹/₂ miles south-east of Hereford, on the B4224 to Fownhope and Ross-on-Wye. Bar meals. Open 11.30 a.m.–2.30 p.m., 6.30–11 p.m.

The Black Swan, MUCH DEWCHURCH
(SO 483 312)

When the iconoclastic vandals of King Henry VIII wrought destruction on the monastic houses in 1536, the inn at the little village of Much Dewchurch was known as the White Swan; when the dust had settled, and the last monk turned out of his church, it had been renamed the Black Swan. This is the story told about the origin of the pub's name, although the symbolism is a little unclear. Perhaps it was frequented by monks or pilgrims on their way from Hereford to the monastic sites at Kilpeck and Abbey Dore, and with the Dissolution the taverner decided to distance his establishment from any reference to the white habits worn by Cistercian monks, to avoid royal disapproval. But perhaps this is too far-fetched, and in any case we cannot be sure that the Black Swan was called such in the sixteenth century, or even if it was a tavern then.

The building itself was certainly standing here while the monasteries were tumbling down, and the unprepossessing exterior hides what is one of the oldest, and most complex, half-timbered buildings in the Welsh Marches. In fact, the Swan shows almost every alteration to befall a medieval timbered house over centuries of changing architectural fashions.

Stripping away the disguises of later years, we can envisage the building as it was when first built, sometime in the fifteenth century. Like all timbered buildings the component parts were shaped and pre-assembled at the carpenter's yard before being taken to the building plot. A stone foundation plinth was laid, and on this was reared the main structural supports – great curved cruck trusses which rose from the ground to the full height of the building. Once these were in place, the smaller side beams and support frames were slotted into their positions, and pegged. Along the junction of the larger beams can be seen strange symbols and notches; these were the marks carved by the carpenter to indicate which piece went where. With the timber 'skeleton' complete, the framed spaces were infilled with vertical poles interlaced with twigs, and then covered in a mixture of clay, manure and straw. Exposed sections of wattle and daub can be seen inside the existing building.

As completed, the house consisted of a central hall open to the roof, which was entered along a cross-passage with opposing doorways. On one side of the passage there were two rooms, probably used only for storage, although one has a more ornate beamed ceiling, and so could have been a private chamber. Only one of the arched doors to these rooms now survives, but a similar pair on the floor above indicates that they must have been reached from the hall by a stair, perhaps with a gallery over the cross-passage. The only form of heating was an open hearth in the middle of the floor, and the smoke wafted its way out of an opening, or louvre, in the roof above.

For all the inadequacies and discomforts the grandiose medieval hall remained in use for many generations. Then, in the early seventeenth century, the owner carried out a series of alterations which almost totally disguised the

Much Dewchurch, the Black Swan: cutaway view *c.* 1650. The medieval hall has been transformed by the addition of chimneys and upper floors, and the presumed inner rooms beyond the hall have been removed

earlier plan. The great space of the hall was reduced by the insertion of an upper floor, and either end of the building was capped by huge masonry turrets containing spacious fireplaces and winding stairs to the upper floors. Some people believe that these were defensible towers dating from the Middle Ages, and that the narrow windows lighting the stairs were used as arrow-slits to guard against the approach of a hostile force from either England or Wales – depending on the sympathies of the occupants. The old cross-passage was no longer used and its doors were turned into windows. Finally, the entire front of the building was encased in stonework, so that now only the rear displays the original timbered walls. More recent works have enlarged the bar area, although sadly in the process a large fireplace with a beautifully carved wooden lintel has been lost. But there is much else to admire here; the lounge retains the original post-and-panel partition with its Tudor-arch doorway – a rare survival, for so often only a row of slots in a ceiling beam indicates where such a partition stood.

On the back of one of the panels is a pattern of shot-holes, said to have been made at the time of the Civil War. According to the story, Cromwell was drinking in the lounge with his cronies, when a disgruntled Royalist soldier took a pot-shot through the window. Had his aim been as good as his intent, then a goodly chunk of British history would have been rewritten. But the shot went wide, the soldier was hanged, and his ghost now walks the Black Swan at night.

Much Dewchurch lies on the B4348, signposted off either the A465 or A49, 6 miles south-west of Hereford. Bar meals. Open 11 a.m.–2.30 p.m., 6.30–11 p.m.

The Harp Inn, OLD RADNOR
(SO 251 591)

New Radnor was 'new' in the thirteenth century, when the Normans refounded the town some miles away from the original Welsh settlement, and now Old Radnor is left very much to itself, a cluster of houses and church on a hill overlooking the Summergill valley. The imposing parish church is renowned for its carved fifteenth-century screen, but less well known is the Harp Inn which stands in the shadow of the tall, battlemented tower. The bare stone renovated exterior is in contrast to the unrestored interior. There is a floor of polished flagstones, some unblackened ceiling beams, and a cross-corner inglenook with a bread oven at the side. Other early features are hidden awaiting further restoration. In the bar there is a high-backed curving settle, an unusual piece of furniture, and just beyond a doorway leads to an elegant farmhouse-style dining room. Charles I is said to have stopped here and complained about the food, but customers can rest assured that things have changed since the seventeenth century.

The hilltop village of Old Radnor lies off the A44 at Walton Green, midway between New Radnor and Kington. Bar snacks and meals, accommodation. Open 12–2.30 p.m., 7–11 p.m.

Boot Inn, ORLETON
(SO 492 672

Before being turned into a public house, the Boot Inn was a butcher's and a shoemaker's shop, and so the origin of the name is explained. Orleton is a little village strung out along the old road from Ludlow to Leominster, now bypassed in part by the B4361. There is a church at one end, a manor house at the other, and in between the Boot Inn. The oldest part is a seventeenth-century half-timbered cottage, with a stone slate roof and a tall, tottering brick chimney. The interior is a most attractive lounge with exposed wattle and daub walls (the panels on the outside have been infilled with brick) and a low beamed ceiling. The more untrustworthy beams have been propped up with baulks to prevent the ceiling from sagging! The wholly brick wing at the side which now houses the bar is a much later addition, though it is graced with a large, old-fashioned inglenook.

The Boot is another example of the 'unit system' where several self-contained dwellings stand close to or adjoin each other; but here it is the smaller, secondary house which is by far the most interesting. It cannot be seen from the pub itself, and many customers may not realize it even exists; but just at the rear of the cottage (and clearly visible from the pleasant beer garden) is a tiny half-timbered building which measures just 8 x 10 ft. It looks for all the world like the proverbial privy at the bottom of the garden, but even a cursory glance at the exterior will reveal that it is undeniably a house. There are windows, a door, a stone fireplace and an asbestos roof (an unfortunate modern addition). This is thought to be one of the smallest houses in Britain, and there is only one room inside, with a diminutive ladder-stair in the corner

Orleton, the Boot Inn: cutaway reconstruction of the tiny seventeenth- or eighteenth-century house beyond the inn

leading up to a bedroom in the loft. Why anyone should trouble to build such a doll's house in the first place is a far bigger puzzle than that posed by the 'unit system' itself. Could it have been a dower house built by an exceptionally stingy husband, or was it for the apprentice of the bootmaker who lived above his shop? Until about twenty years ago this house was inhabited, but it is now disused; the interior is full of junk, and the wattle walls are crumbling. The brick chimney has already fallen. Fortunately help may be at hand since the present landlord intends to preserve this remarkable hovel.

Orleton lies just off the B4361 road to Leominster, about 4 miles south-west of Ludlow. Alternately take the main A49 to Leominster, then turn right at Woofferton Cross along the B4362. After 1½ miles a left turn leads to Orleton. Bar snacks and meals. Open 11 a.m.–11 p.m.

PEMBRIDGE

(SO 390 581)

A walk down Pembridge's single main street is like a step or two back in time. Everywhere you look there are magpie houses with red tile or grey slate roofs, lofty brick and stone chimneys, some leaning tipsily as if on the move to another village. Pembridge has more old houses than new, in total contrast to so many other towns and villages where one or two half-timbered buildings may be all that remains of the medieval settlement. And Pembridge displays for the passer-by over six centuries of domestic architecture. If one could wish for a more impressive castle ruin than the feeble earthworks beside the graveyard, then at least the noble parish church makes up for this deficiency. Work on this largely fourteenth-century building was reputedly delayed by an outbreak of the Black Death. But more impressive than the cathedral-like interior is the famous detached belltower, squatting like a pagoda among the graves. The inside is a dark, stony cave, with a forest of oak pillars supporting the belfry. The village was the scene of much fighting in the Civil War, and shot-holes can be seen in the thick wooden door.

From the churchyard gate a lane winds down to the cobbled market-place where once salesmen and wool merchants carried out transactions, stopping only for refreshment at the adjacent New Inn. The scene is still much the same today, though the old market hall has lost its timbered upper half. The inn now dominates the market-place and what might be called the centre of the town. Half-timbered houses huddle around, but none can compete with that splendid façade crowned at either end with jettied bays. The New Inn is said to have replaced an older tavern in the village, hence the name, in the fourteenth century. But this cannot be substantiated on architectural grounds, and all the details point to an early seventeenth-century date. Alas, the story that a peace treaty was signed here in 1471, after the battle of Mortimers Cross, must be consigned to folklore.

The building has a fairly simple plan – a central hall flanked by a kitchen and parlour, with bedchambers and guest-rooms on the upper floor. Symmetry is reserved for the front façade, and the rear is a cluster of tall stone chimneys, gabled turrets and some modern additions. The interior is a wealth of dark wood, and wattle and daub partitions. All the doorways have square heads, not arches as in a genuine medieval building. A large wooden settle with a curved back is said to have formed part of the seating at a local cockpit, dismantled and brought here when the bloodthirsty sport was banned in 1849. Due to the sloping ground a cellar was constructed under the lounge, but if the stories are true then it fulfilled a less mundane function than a cool store. Prisoners were kept locked up here before being tried for some misdemeanour in the court room on the first floor. Perhaps one of the miserable wretches incarcerated in this dark hole died there, for the inn is reputedly haunted by the ghost of a red-coat soldier. The shade of a young girl has also been seen, flitting to and fro about the rooms; but this charming spectre only appears to women!

Further along the road to Leominster stands the Pembridge Inn, until recently known as the Greyhound and originally as the King's House. Although the New Inn has pride of place in many guidebooks as the 'oldest' pub in town, the Pembridge pre-dates it by about a hundred years. Photographs taken earlier this century show a drab and undistinguished building, but the thick layers of paint and cement rendering have been stripped away to reveal the glories of half-timbering. The inn dates from the beginning of the sixteenth century, and the close timber framing is a typically early feature; so too is the Tudor-arch doorway (now blocked) with a richly carved head. Notice too the ornamental posts and corbels which add a touch of refinement to the jettied front. The basic features are repeated around the back, but all the fine carvings are reserved for the front of the house, to impress upon passers-by the wealth and social aspirations of the owners.

The blocked door led on to a cross-passage between twin service rooms and a hall – a classic medieval plan; but here there were no smoky rooms open to the rafters, for the upper floor is an original feature and a fine stone fireplace, not an open hearth, provided warmth for the family. The existing stack must be an insertion, since it intrudes on to the cross-passage, and the original fireplace may have been in the side wall where an entire length of half-timbering is missing. Most of the upper floor was taken up by a second hall, open to the roof, but the noble proportions of this chamber have been lost by the insertion of an attic and partitioned rooms. These alterations may have been carried out when the east end of the house was remodelled in the mid-sixteenth century. The much plainer details of this phase contrast with the richly carved timberwork of the older hall. Clearly the builders of the original house had considerable pride in their new home.

Pembridge lies about 6 miles east of Leominster on the A44 to Kington. Bar snacks and meals. Open 11 a.m.–3 p.m., 6–11 p.m. Stop Press: the Pembridge Inn has recently closed.

The Radnorshire Arms, PRESTEIGNE
(SO 314 644)

Eight miles north-west of Pembridge, in the valley of the Lugg, stands the border town of Presteigne. Here too there are half-timbered buildings lining the main streets but, sadly, these are only the fortunate few survivors of a once greater number. The place-name is thought to derive from old English 'priest's house', and there was certainly a settlement here before the Normans arrived; remains of Saxon masonry have been detected in the medieval parish church. In the seventeenth century, according to folklore, a group of thirteen parsons gathered at the church to rid the area of the ghost of Black Vaughan of Hergest Court. When the evil spirit appeared twelve of the men fainted in terror, but the last resolutely carried on with the exorcism and reduced the apparition to the size of a fly. It was then trapped in a snuff-box and buried under a large stone in a pond.

No such dramatic ghost stories concern the Radnorshire Arms, though there are other legends associated with this 370-year-old coaching inn. The immaculately kept timber-framed building is an imposing testament to the confidence and aspirations of the Stuart gentry in Wales. If you ignore the Victorian accretions at the rear, the main part of the inn has survived the centuries relatively unscathed. Beyond the front door is a cross-passage leading through to the main staircase and added rear rooms. To the left is the 'Oak

Presteigne, the Radnorshire Arms: a fine Renaissance house dated 1616, with more modern extensions at the rear

Room', aptly named since the half-timbered walls are lined with elegant panelling, and leaded windows overlook the formal gardens. On the right is the lounge-bar, a surprisingly dark room, heavy with carved beams and oak panelling. Rows of mullioned windows provide some light, but here it is all too easy to imagine some spectre gliding out of the dark woodwork to greet the unsuspecting guest. During renovations to the building in the last century, a priest's hole was discovered behind some panelling, along with the diary of a Catholic who had sheltered there for two years. Some of the panels are claimed to have been damaged by looters searching the inn for hidden treasure.

The Radnorshire Arms was built in 1616, as a date on the splendid porch informs us, although it did not become an inn until the end of the eighteenth century. It was reputedly the home of Sir Christopher Hatton, Queen Elizabeth's favourite courtier, although he died in 1591. Similarly the story that the inn was the work of John Bradshaw, one of the men involved in the trial and execution of Charles I, can also be discounted. Though a John Bradshaw owned the house in the seventeenth century, the regicide was a Cheshire man who would only have been aged fourteen when the inn was built. Bradshaw fortunately died just before the return of King Charles II, although this did not prevent his remains from being unearthed and hung on a gibbet. If the story that Bradshaw built the house were true it would be particularly ironic, since one of the guests who reputedly stayed here was King Charles himself!

Presteigne town stands at the junction of the B4362 and B4355 roads midway between Kington and Knighton, and about 6 miles west of Mortimer's Cross on the A4110. Bar snacks and meals, accommodation. Open 11 a.m.–11 p.m.

The New Inn, ST OWEN'S CROSS
(SO 539 247)

When the inspectors of the Royal Commission on Ancient Monuments visited the New Inn in the early 1930s, they were misled into thinking that this was a stone-built house of the seventeenth century. The date is very likely correct, but recent renovations have proved that the 'stone' walls are in fact timber-framed, disguised by a thick coat of rendering. Now that the layers have been stripped away from the exterior façade, you can see the latticework of decayed timbers underneath. Thankfully the restorers avoided the temptation to blacken the beams, and the wattle and daub panels have been painted yellow; something of a contrast to the generally accepted image of a 'black and white' house, but some experts believe that many walls would have been similarly treated, rather than painted stark white. In any case, the daub surface would never have stayed clean and gleaming for long in the British climate.

Before many of the alterations and refurbishments disguised the layout and proportions of the inn, this would have been a large and imposing timbered building. It was built to a lobby-entry plan, and so the rough stone wall facing customers when they open the front door is the side wall of the main fireplace. Note the tiny alcove by the door – perhaps an early wall safe? Much of the former grandeur of this building is still reflected by the surviving panelling and carved beams in the guest-rooms upstairs. The old hall (now the bar) is still heated by a log fire in the large stone inglenook. At the time of my visit the barman was wrestling manfully with an awkwardly large log which refused to sit on the hearth, and the smoke did not always escape up the chimney – giving more than a hint of life in a smoggy medieval hall!

The New Inn stands at the junction of the B4521 with the A4137 Hereford road, about 3 miles west of Ross-on-Wye. Bar snacks and meals, accommodation. Open 12–3 p.m., 6–11 p.m.

The Lough Pool, SELLACK
(SO 558 267)

This is not one of the easiest pubs to find, nor are there any helpful signposts to point the way. The building has stood in rural isolation for about three hundred years and its history is as untroubled as the surface of the nearby pond which gives the inn its name. But few other pubs can lay claim to such a tranquil and idyllic setting, and even if its near neighbour, the Cottage of Content (p. 80), can hold its place as the classic 'picture-postcard' country inn, then at least the Lough Pool runs a close second.

Inevitably there have been some modern alterations to the building, but it is still the original seventeenth-century timbered cottage which catches the eye. Brick has replaced wattle and daub, and there are new windows and doors; but inside little else has changed. A log fire burns in the cavernous inglenook and flagstones grace the floor. The more crooked ceiling beams have been propped up by tree trunks. There is a new restaurant extension at the rear which blends in with the older work, although the stone end wing is too much of a contrast. Until recently the pub was called the 'Love Pool', but the present landlord has reverted to the older spelling, which is said to derive from an Irish word for bog. Certainly there is nothing overly romantic about the pond, covered with duckweed and shaded by mournful willows.

The Lough Pool is situated beside a minor road to Hoarwithy, 3 miles north-east of Ross-on-Wye. From Ross take the A49 to Hereford, and turn right at Winters Cross, following the signs to Sellack. After about a mile there is a crossroads; turn left, and the pub will be seen in a valley bottom on the left. Bar snacks and meals. Open 12–2.30 p.m., 7–11 p.m.

WEOBLEY

(SO 403 517)

Weobley is almost a monument in itself; the jewel in Herefordshire's crown of black-and-white villages. A surfeit of medieval, sixteenth- and seventeenth-century half-timbered houses confront the passer-by, and the only stone building here of any significance is the parish church. In contrast to nearby Pembridge (see p. 101) the church is innocuously sited on low-lying ground, drawing attention to itself with the aid of a tall tower and graceful spire. Inside is a remarkable monument to one James Tomkyns who fathered thirty-three children, all but one of whom survived into adulthood. Another memorial commemorates Colonel Birch, who rose through the ranks in Cromwell's army to become an MP of the borough, and Governor of Hereford. He wisely turned sides on Cromwell's death and welcomed the Stuart successor.

Unfortunately little is left of Earl Roger de Lacy's castle, but between the earthworks of that vanished stronghold and the church there is six centuries of domestic architecture to gaze at. Many of the street-front houses had oversailing upper floors, a feature more commonly found in built-up areas where space was at a premium. In such a rural setting as Weobley with a broad main street it might seem unwarranted, but in fact the flower garden running down the middle of the road is the site of the market hall and a row of houses which burnt down in 1860. The town was very much more cramped in previous centuries.

One of the earliest, and most impressive, of Weobley's survivors is the Red Lion, which stands next to the lane leading down to the church. At the time of writing it is closed, but one hopes this unfortunate situation will be remedied before long. Photographs taken in the early part of this century show that the Lion was then a drab and undistinguished building, but when the thick coat of render was stripped away all the timber details were brought to light. The two-storeyed corner block is the only surviving part of a fourteenth-century house, the adjoining hall having been rebuilt in the seventeenth century and the lower walls infilled with brick. There may have been a second cross-wing at the opposite end of the hall, and in fact a very similar building survives next to the Unicorn Inn. The few remaining carved windows and doors testify to the high quality of carpentry lavished on the original house.

The Salutation Inn is tucked away at the top end of the main street, where the ground falls steeply away to the west. As a result the pub is built on different levels, and from the outside looks as if it is about to tumble down the hillside. Most of the upper bar has been rebuilt in brick, but the lower lounge is a half-timbered cottage with a stone inglenook at one end.

Weobley, the Red Lion: the end wing is all that survives of a fourteenth-century hall. Note the cruck-framed building in the background

The nearby Unicorn Inn has a stern, imposing, well-proportioned façade, but some light relief is provided by its lopsided, multi-gabled neighbour. The Unicorn is very much a local's local, with a fairly unmodernized interior. The lounge has a stone fireplace and a heavy beamed ceiling. An unusual collection of beer mats already covers most of the available ceiling space and is now slowly creeping down the walls.

Weobley lies just off the A4112 between Hay-on-Wye and Leominster, about 6 miles south-west of Leominster. Bar snacks and meals. Open 11 a.m.–3 p.m., 7–11 p.m.; Saturday: 11 a.m.–11 p.m.

Butcher's Arms, WOOLHOPE
(SO 616 357)

First a word of warning: do not rush headlong into this pub in search of a drink, for the ceiling beams are only 5½ ft high in places! The oft-displayed label 'Duck or Grouse' was surely coined with the Butcher's Arms in mind.

But as is so often the case, such warped ceilings add to the charm and atmosphere of an old country pub, and since the beams have been in place for some 350 years, it is hardly fair to expect perfect timberwork.

The Butcher's Arms lies some distance away from the village of Woolhope, aloof and isolated in a gentle valley bottom. The village itself was once a manor belonging to Wulviva, sister of Lady Godiva, who granted it to Hereford Cathedral in the eleventh century. It is her more famous sibling, however, who appears in a modern stained-glass window in the church. From the roadside the pub is a photogenic cluster of crisp black and white timbering, tall brick chimneys, and varying rooflines and dormers covered in bright red pantiles. The only major alteration to have befallen this seventeenth-century cottage in recent years is a rear extension, which leads to a patio overlooking the garden.

There are now two doors into the pub, but customers should enter from the roadside (if only for the sake of architectural propriety), since this door opens on to the original cross-passage. On the left are private rooms, while a door on the right of the passage leads to the bar. This was formerly the hall, and the low, dark and cramped appearance of the original room has been greatly altered by the recent renovations. Light floods into the little room through the patio doors; and if the purist objects to such large areas of glass (there is still one unglazed original window in the adjoining shed), then at least the low ceiling provides some authenticity. Beyond the hall is the lounge, which must have been the early kitchen since there is a bake-oven in one side of the inglenook. There is said to be a blocked up 'secret room' between the hall and kitchen fireplaces, and there is certainly some truth in this, for the gap between the two projecting chimneys has been filled with a roofed-over lean-to. This may be the remains of a corn-drying kiln, or else a large bake-oven, rather than a hidden room – particularly since it is so obvious from outside! On the pub walls are photographs taken earlier this century, depicting events in the agricultural life of the village, but perhaps more interesting is a framed article from a 1960s copy of the *Hereford Evening News* which mentions the pub's most unusual regular. This was a mongrel dog called Nigger who could taste and distinguish between draught and bottled beer, but preferred a drop of mild!

The pub lies beyond Woolhope village, on a signposted minor road which can be followed from the B4224 Hereford to Ross-on-Wye road, at either Mordiford or Fownhope. Bar snacks and meals, accommodation. Open 11.30 a.m.–2.30 p.m., 6.30–11 p.m.

Additional inns and taverns

Aberllynfi, Three Cocks Hotel (SO 173 378)

Bredwardine, Red Lion (SO 332 444)

Gladestry, Royal Oak (SO 233 552)

Llowes, Radnor Arms (SO 193 417)

Lyonshall, Royal George (SO 337 556)

Michaelchurch Escley, Bridge Inn (SO 318 341)

Yarpole, Bell Inn (SO 469 649)

4. MID-WALES AND THE MARCHES

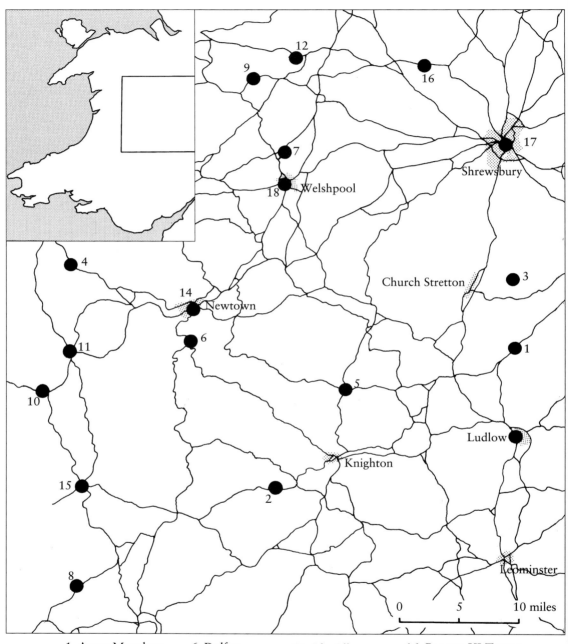

1. Aston Munslow
2. Bleddfa
3. Cardington
4. Carno
5. Clun
6. Dolfor
7. Guilsfield
8. Llanafan
9. Llanfechain
10. Llangurig
11. Llanidloes
12. Llanyblodwel
13. Ludlow
14. Newtown
15. Rhayader
16. Ruyton-XI-Towns
17. Shrewsbury
18. Welshpool

Swan Inn, ASTON MUNSLOW
(SO 512 867)

A cluster of stone chimneys and timbered gables heaped higgledy-piggledy on a rise above the road announces the Swan Inn to travellers passing through Corve Dale. Dick Turpin is claimed to have been a customer here, although that was in the days when he was a humble butcher's apprentice, before his infamous career took off. This valley sandwiched between Wenlock Edge and the Clee Hills has its share of picturesque villages and country pubs, but the Swan is one of the best.

Across the road is a photogenic row of timbered cottages, more orderly and symmetrical than the Swan, but if you strip away the additions of later years you'll find that the inn started life as a simple and unambitious farmhouse of *c.* 1600; a building which now forms the central core of the pub. Walls once exposed to the elements now form partitions between rooms well inside the

Aston Munslow, the Swan Inn: reconstruction of the probable appearance of the inn *c.* 1600. The storeyed bay on the right appears to have been an addition to the hall, and served to emphasize its importance

building. Nevertheless many of the original features still survive; upstairs low and hefty timbers support the sagging roof, while both ground-floor rooms (the original rooms – there are now several sprouting off the older parts) have large stone fireplaces. The hearth in the rear bar-lounge has an oven at the side, so this room was probably the kitchen. The cross-beamed hall is unusually narrow, but as if to make up for this deficiency there is an impressive storeyed bay at one end. Such bays usually functioned as a porch, forming a grand entry to the house (see, for instance, the Radnorshire Arms, Presteigne), but here it seems to have been little more than an extension of the hall, with windows to light the high table. Clearly the owner felt the need to add a bit of architectural class to his home.

Several generations later another owner felt the same need, and built a large stone parlour wing adjoining the kitchen. This now forms an elegant dining room. This was clearly the owner's pride and joy, for the ceiling beams are neatly carved and there are plaster decorations around the window. There is a cast-iron fireback in the hall, bearing a fleur-de-lis and the date 1691, which very likely records these alterations. Further work carried out in the eighteenth and nineteenth centuries practically engulfed the older hall, although parts of the structure are clearly visible. Tradition places a date of 1350 on the inn, but nothing structural survives from the Middle Ages. Slightly more credible is the story of a boisterous farmer who was once refused a drink by the landlord and stormed out of the pub in anger. He returned a few minutes later on horseback, charged up the steps and through the door, and galloped around the hall to the understandable consternation of everyone present!

The village lies about 7 miles north of Ludlow, beside the B4368 road from Craven Arms to Bridgenorth. Bar snacks and meals. Open 12–3 p.m., 7–11 p.m.

The Hundred House Inn, BLEDDFA
(SO 207 684)

Monaughty is the architectural gem of Bleddfa, one of the great houses of Wales, standing alongside the main road to Knighton. Motorists have a good view of this sixteenth- and seventeenth-century mansion before approaching, or upon leaving, the tiny village. But another, less imposing, building here has a history as well. From as early as 1524 until 1867 the court of the Hundred

Townships of Cefnllys met at the village inn to discuss legal matters and the affairs of the parish, and to settle any petty misdemeanours. Even the churchwardens had few qualms about holding their meetings here. The inevitably named Hundred House is now solely an inn, and no longer are wrongdoers likely to be sentenced to death here, and hanged at Monaughty.

The court-house attended by the ruthless circuit judges does not survive, for the existing building is entirely seventeenth century. It was probably constructed in the latter half of that century, when the concept of the 'central plan', with greater emphasis on privacy and better circulation between rooms, was filtering down from the larger houses to the smaller. The present lounge and bar occupy two large rooms on either side of a central passageway, which contains a stair to the cellar and first floor. The plan is identical to many modern cottages, but there are still some archaic features, such as the heavy beamed ceiling and large inglenooks – one with the outlines of a blocked oven in its side. A later extension now houses a dining area and games room.

The new owners are unsure if the place is genuinely haunted, although the ghost of a medieval lady has reputedly been seen, and dogs and cats are said to take a dislike to the hall fireplace, howling at it and running away!

The village of Bleddfa lies 5 miles south-west of Knighton, on the A488 to Rhayader. Bar meals, accommodation. Open 11 a.m.–11 p.m.; Winter: 11 a.m.–3 p.m., 6–11 p.m.

The Royal Oak, CARDINGTON
(SO 505 953)

The Royal Oak at Cardington may be associated by name with Charles II, but the sign swinging outside depicts a pagan face, wreathed in green leaves, peering out of an oak tree. This brings to mind not so much the 'merry monarch' but the Green Man of ancient May Day festivities. And this tradition is continued inside, where a length of aged timber from the church has been carved into a Celtic-style face by a local craftsman. There is also a more familiar royal face on display here, a photograph of Prince Edward taken a few years ago when the prince and participants in the Duke of Edinburgh Award Scheme stopped briefly at the Royal Oak.

From the modern to the old: although the Oak boasts a fifteenth-century date there is little evidence (as usual) to support such an early origin, and the surviving features would not be out of place in the seventeenth century. There is a huge gable fireplace, a heavy cross-beamed ceiling and a half-timbered partition separating the hall (now the bar) from the entrance passage and upper lounge. The pub was built into the church-crowned hillside, so that there is a change of levels inside, and all the rooms on the upper side of the bar have been modernized. The photogenic exterior is a cluster of tipsy dormers and sagging eaves, in summer buried under masses of flowers in hanging baskets.

Cardington lies between Church Stretton and Wenlock Edge, and is best reached off the B4371 road to Much Wenlock. Alternatively there is a signposted route through country lanes from Leebotwood on the A49 Shrewsbury to Ludlow road. Bar meals. Open 12–2.30 p.m., 7–11 p.m., closed Monday lunchtimes, November until Easter.

The Aleppo Merchant, CARNO
(SN 963 964)

The Aleppo Merchant stands guard at the heart of Carno village, a huddled pile of grey slate roofs and whitewashed walls. It shares its location with the parish church of St John, once the property of the Knights Hospitaller, whose medieval hospice provided rest and accommodation for tired wayfarers and pilgrims. Now, centuries later, the Aleppo has taken on the task. The maritime association of the inn is linked to a sea captain who retired here around 1850, and renamed the pub after his merchant vessel which traded between Liverpool and Aleppo in Syria. A splendid painting of the ship hangs in the lounge. According to some tales the captain was a far from respectable character, and his wealth was gained in very dubious circumstances.

The building itself was standing long before the nineteenth century, and there is a sign outside which claims a date of 1632. While there seems to be no evidence for such a precise date, it cannot be far wrong. Originally the building would have been entirely half-timbered except for the gable ends which contained the big fireplaces and were, for obvious reasons, built of stone. The captain or his successors replaced almost all the old woodwork with more durable masonry, but inside the elegant panelled lounge are some original oak beams and a few surviving half-timbered panels. Black and white

Plasnewydd House, on the hillside just east of the village and visible from the road, gives a good impression of how striking the Aleppo Merchant would have appeared centuries ago.

The inn stands alongside the A470 Newtown to Machynlleth road, midway between Caersws and Llanbrynmair. Bar snacks and meals, accommodation. Open 12–2.30 p.m., 6–11 p.m.

The Sun Inn, CLUN
(SO 302 809)

'Clunton, Clunbury, Clungunford and Clun, are the quietest places under the sun' runs the familiar and oft-repeated jingle. But it was not always so in the past, and numerous monuments testify that this sparsely populated area of Shropshire was bitterly fought over by natives and invaders alike. Several Iron Age forts crown the summits of surrounding hills, including Caer Caradoc, one of the places where Caractacus is said to have made his last stand against the Romans in AD 50. Offa's Dyke runs across country just two miles to the west, and the numerous 'mottes' marked on OS maps show that the Normans were busy consolidating their land gains in the eleventh and twelfth centuries. Beside the little village itself stand the impressive earthworks of Robert de Say's stronghold. When the castle was held by the Fitz Alans in the twelfth century they added stone defences, including a glowering keep precariously perched halfway down the side of the mound.

Once the military presence of the Normans had been imposed on the area, a small town was established just beyond the gates of the castle. This was probably meant to replace an older Saxon settlement clustered about the church on the opposite side of the river. The two 'towns' are now linked by a delightful late-medieval packhorse bridge, with cutwaters and recesses for pedestrians. Since this was the main road from Shrewsbury to Knighton, walkers had to keep a watchful eye on the traffic – thus the saying arose: 'whoever crosses Clun bridge comes home sharper than he went'. Once across the river the road abruptly forks left, to Bishop's Castle (passing the old Town Hall, now a museum), and right, to Craven Arms. Here on the left stands the Sun Inn, one of the few survivors of the town's former sixteen public houses.

If Clun is one of the quietest places under the sun, then the Sun is not always the quietest place in Clun; but should the small bar become too packed, then there is always room to spread out in the charming lounge. The inn itself is a cruck-truss building, probably of sixteenth-century date, although the plain, rendered exterior gives no hint of this. Only from inside is it possible to appreciate the origin of the inn, with the lower halves of the crucks visible in the side walls curving up and disappearing beyond the inserted ceiling. On some of the exposed panelling in the lounge can be seen the remains of a simple floral pattern painted on the wattle and daub walls in the seventeenth century. Such mural designs are rare survivals, more often lost or hidden, and awaiting rediscovery by stripping away layer upon layer of whitewash.

There is a tradition that the inn was originally a barn or stable, serving a manor house, now a shop, across the road. In converting such a building into a dwelling all that was needed was to build a fireplace, and set up beams to support an upper floor. The fireplace opening has been greatly reduced in size, but wooden benches are still arranged around the hearth, just as they would have been in the days when the only warmth to be had was from a sputtering fire in the cavernous inglenook. Beyond the bar are guest-rooms and a restaurant which, within living memory, was a bakery.

I visited Clun on May Day, and found the square and riverbank lined with people. This was all part of the traditional May Day rituals, when the Green Man is dressed up and people dance around the Maypole – ceremonies which have their origins in our pre-Christian past. But here at Clun the festivities entailed floating yellow plastic ducks down the river!

Clun lies at the junction of the B4368 with the A488 Knighton to Bishop's Castle road, about 6 miles west of Craven Arms. Bar snacks and meals, accommodation. Open 11 a.m.–3 p.m. (4 p.m. on Saturdays), 6–11 p.m.

The Dolfor Inn, DOLFOR
(SO 106 874)

High up in a fold of the Kerry hills stands the little village of Dolfor, a group of farms and cottages clustered around a Victorian brick and terracotta church. The A483 snakes through Dolfor on its way down into the Severn valley, but for centuries this busy highway was a rutted dirt track used only by farmers, drovers and a few hardy travellers. The inn started life in the early seventeenth century as a farmhouse, and if any beer was brewed here it would have been drunk by the family and their neighbours; but with the gradual improvement in the road network more travellers passed through the district, and the farmhouse opened its doors as a hostelry.

Today the inn is a long low building with a row of tiny dormers rising above the eaves. The tarmac forecourt is enclosed by renovated nineteenth-century farm buildings, and the whole looks pristine and new. But beneath the roughcast walls there is brick, and beneath the brick the fossilized remains of the original half-timbered house. From inside the aged wooden framework is more obvious, and the only part originally built from stone is the central chimney-stack with its back-to-back fireplaces. The main bar is housed in the old hall, a large room on the right upon entering. Slots in the beams show that some partitions have been taken down, and there were two small rooms where the pool table now stands. The more insecure beams have been propped up with reused timbers brought from an old warehouse in Newtown. The smaller bar at the other end of the building has been enlarged at some time, and the partly dismantled end walls now separate the bar from a comfortable lounge and dining area. A collection of old prints and fishing flies adorn the walls. During the last century landowners would gather in this room four times a year to collect rents from their tenants. What a dread event that must have been: no doubt the innkeeper made a tidy sum supplying the hard-working farmers with plenty of drinks to fortify their spirits!

Dolfor lies about 3 miles south of Newtown, along the A483 to Llandrindod. Bar meals, accommodation. Open 11 a.m.–2.30 p.m., 6–11 p.m.; Sunday: 12–2.30 p.m., 7–11 p.m.

The Oak Inn, GUILSFIELD

(SJ 217 116)

The village of Guilsfield displays for the passer-by a fine collection of over three centuries of domestic architecture; half-timbered seventeenth-century buildings, stone Georgian and Victorian houses, and more up-to-date constructions in brick and concrete. Oldest of all is the medieval parish church with its magnificent interior crowned by a sixteenth-century painted roof. Around 1830 Samuel Lewis noted 'several genteel residences near the village, among which the splendid mansion of Garth claims particular notice'. Alas, this pinnacled extravaganza was demolished in 1947, robbing Guilsfield of its

Guilsfield, the Oak Inn: this cutaway view of the seventeenth-century house shows the presumed timber-framed fireplace in the hall

most outrageous architectural monument. Another casualty was Palladian Trawscoed Hen, burnt in 1858 and finally knocked down in 1925. But there are still a number of attractive half-timbered buildings in the vicinity, including Llyswen, Broniarth Hall, and the Oak Inn.

For a country pub the Oak has a surprisingly large car-park, but then the building itself is surprisingly large, made even more roomy by modern additions. Whoever built this house in the early seventeenth century was no impoverished farmer but a landowner of some standing, with enough cash to invest in a substantial home for his descendants. Unusually for Montgomeryshire the house was built to a hearth-passage plan, rather than a lobby-entry, so that the hall (now the bar) was entered along a passage from behind the main fireplace.

Guilsfield, the Oak Inn: although the roof has been raised in recent times, the line of the steeper seventeenth-century roof can be seen at the gable end

There were four large rooms on the ground floor alone, and a rear kitchen wing was added some years later. Before then any cooking would have been carried out in the hall fireplace. Local craftsmen carved the heavy oak ceiling beams with a variety of decorative 'stops', and all the doors had arched heads, only one of which survives today. The upper floor was a low, dark attic used only for sleeping, but in the eighteenth century the roof was raised and more windows were added to improve the accommodation. The line of the earlier roof can clearly be seen in the surviving timbered gable. There were further alterations in more recent times when the kitchen and lounge were extended, but a photograph taken in 1914, and on display in the bar, shows the original appearance of the inn before these works were carried out.

Everywhere inside there is dark oak, with slots and peg-holes on many beams showing where some partitions have been taken down. Both bar and lounge are comfortable, light and spacious rooms, but for all its fine carpentry the interior would have been dark and claustrophobic in the seventeenth century. The only light came from low windows which may, or may not, have been graced with glass, depending on the financial resources of the owner. The only heat was provided by the main fireplace, although the existing hearth is modern and a nook compared to its cavernous counterpart. The lounge was probably used as a parlour, although it is said to have been a stable – but surely no homeowner would have paid a carpenter to spend hours carving the beams if they were to be admired only by horses!

Guilsfield lies 2½ miles north of Welshpool off the A490 to Llanfyllin. Bar snacks and meals. Open 11 a.m.–3 p.m., 6–11 p.m.

The Red Lion, LLANAFAN FAWR
(SN 968 557)

'Llanavan full of hills, whose plains are trod by none but idle swains' runs an eighteenth-century jingle, and so it is hardly surprising to find the village and church of Llanafan Fawr nestling on a hilltop in this remote and hilly district of Powys. 'Village' may sound grand to describe the scatter of farms and a castle mound surrounding St Afan's church, and the Red Lion has unfortunately been ignored by early antiquarians. In the twelfth century Gerald of Wales recounted a story about a hunter who was struck blind after thoughtlessly sleeping overnight with his dogs in the church; and six centuries later Theophilus Jones compiled a history of Breconshire, but drew attention only to the church and the larger houses in the parish. But would early travellers have appreciated the age of this building just from the outside?

Today the Red Lion has the appearance of a quaint stone cottage with whitewashed walls, low eaves crowned with dormers, and a solid chimney-stack rising high over the sagging roofline. Once inside some of the eccentricities of the building are explained; the roof is so low because the house never had an original upper floor. Embedded in the walls are the curving blades of cruck trusses, and these, apart from a short length of half-timbered walling beside the bar, are all that remain of the original medieval house. The massive timbers were raised into place during the reign of Henry Tudor, and the simple hall with its open plan and central hearth probably survived little altered until the seventeenth century, when the owners decided to modernize their archaic dwelling. They kept the trusses to support the roof, but put in an upper floor with dormers, rebuilt the half-timbered walls with stone, and replaced the smoky hearth with a large stone fireplace. In the following century a new parlour and rear kitchen wing were added.

For generations this was Llanafan Fawr farm and it is only in fairly recent

Llanafan, the Red Lion: reconstruction of the hall. The drawing shows the characteristic features of medieval buildings: the unglazed windows, open hearth, smoke vent in the roof. The central cruck truss is obscured at present, and so the form of the upper part is conjectural. In the seventeenth century an upper floor was inserted into the hall

times that it became used as an inn. Until recently it was closed, but a new tenant has reopened the pub, and is currently engaged in a slow restoration process. Pumps have now been installed and so the customer is denied the experience of drinking beer drawn by hand from casks, but the lounge is still more like a farmhouse kitchen than a pub. There are some horsebrasses and blackened beams (prerequisites, it seems, of any 'olde worlde' pub today), but also old settles and tables, a Welsh dresser, linoleum floor (covering old flagstones), a spit rack over the fire, and a mantelpiece bearing a row of willow pattern plates. All the walls are plain papered, and the large boulders on which the crucks are seated are the only stonework visible. The great inglenook has been partly blocked, and a bread-oven in its side covered up. All the stonework is shrouded in layer upon layer of wallpaper (as was all the timber until recently), but the outlines of the carved jamb stones and massive lintel can still be traced.

A quandary facing the new owner is whether to strip away the paper and reopen the old hearth to its former extent, or leave everything as it is. It must be remembered that the interiors of old houses were rarely left with bare stone showing; since glass was so costly and windows generally small, the occupants needed as much light as possible. A coat of plaster and whitewash over the stonework would have brightened up the interior immensely. And so the Red Lion stands as a memorial to five centuries of house building, from its origin as a humble timber hall of the Middle Ages, to the more comfortable dwelling of Cromwell's day, and finally through to the homely Welsh cottage interior which many people remember and some still inhabit.

The Red Lion lies about 4 miles north-west of Builth Wells, on the B4358 Newbridge-on-Wye to Beulah road. From Builth take the A470 Rhayader road to Newbridge, where a left turn leads to Llanafan. Open 11 a.m.–11 p.m. (Easter to September); 11 a.m.–2 p.m., 6–11 p.m. (September to Easter).

The Plas-yn-Dinas Inn, LLANFECHAIN
(SJ 189 203)

The B4393 completely misses the old centre of Llanfechain village, and a short detour is needed to reach the parish church and its attendant cluster of stone and timber houses. Just beside the raised mound of the churchyard stands the Plas-yn-Dinas Inn; the curious name can be translated as 'the place of the fort', perhaps a reference to the prominent motte and bailey castle a short distance away beside the Llanfyllin road. There is also a Plas-yn-Dinas earthwork in the neighbouring Vyrnwy valley. Whatever the provenance of the name, the inn was constructed in the last years of the reign of Elizabeth I, though there have been some additions since then.

When first built this was a fairly ambitious timber-framed house comprising a hall and inner room (now the bar), with a right-angled parlour wing at one end. The half-timbered dividing walls still survive in part to mark out the various rooms, though the biggest change of all has been the removal of the central stone chimney with its back-to-back fireplaces – only a gap in the beamed ceiling showing where it stood! All the original ground-floor parts of the building are accessible to customers, and it is worth noting that the finer carpentry details were reserved for the parlour wing, so often the showpiece of a house. At one time part of the inn was used as a butcher's shop, but careful restoration has removed all traces of that venture and, at the time of writing (1992) further extensions are planned which testify to the continued popularity of this country pub.

Llanfechain lies just off the B4393 road from Llansantffraid to Llanfyllin. From Welshpool follow the A490 to Llanfyllin for 8 miles, to where a signposted right turn leads to Llanfechain; alternatively take the A483 from Oswestry to Llansantffraid. Bar meals. Open 11 a.m.–3 p.m. (Saturday: 12–3 p.m.), 6.30–11 p.m.(Sunday: 7–10.30 p.m.).

The Blue Bell Inn, LLANGURIG

(SN 907 799)

When the *Cambrian Traveller's Guide* was published in 1813 the village of Llangurig received a far from favourable entry: 'melancholy and wretched and offering no accommodation'. This is no longer true, and apart from the Blue Bell itself there are other guest-houses here catering for visitors who wish to sample the fishing, golfing, shooting, mountain walking, and pony trekking activities on offer. The guide also expressed frustration at the 'inexpressibly laborious road', and that was certainly no mean-spirited gripe, for the condition of many roads in nineteenth-century rural Wales was atrocious, to say the least. Even today the road west to Aberystwyth passes through some of the bleakest areas of mid-Wales, with only a few scattered farms dotting the landscape, and here and there the remains of old lead mine workings.

It may well have been the remoteness and seclusion of this valley which attracted St Curig here in the sixth century, and his church, much rebuilt by the Victorians, stands guard at the west end of the village. A plaque in the nave commemorates the visit here, in 1917, of Prince Albert, the future King George VI. Opposite the lich-gate stands the Blue Bell Inn, a welcoming respite for the traveller coming down from the high road over the slopes of

Llangurig, the Blue Bell: a late eighteenth-century lobby-entry house

Pumlumon. According to tradition the Inn was built in the sixteenth century to house the workers restoring the parish church. The same story is told about the Pandy Inn (p. 80), but despite its archaic plan the Blue Bell was probably built as late as the eighteenth century. This is a classic lobby-entry house with back-to-back fireplaces, and closely resembles both the Dolfor Inn (p. 118) and the Royal Head (p. 126) except that the walls were built from stone and were never half-timbered.

Once through the front door there is a sharp turn into either the lounge on the right, or the bar. This was the original hall, with a heavy beamed ceiling, flagstone floor, a large inglenook and an equally impressive settle. There was another room beyond the hall but only slots on the ceiling beam show where the partition was taken down. All the other rooms and buildings clustered about the old house are later additions, and include a games room and hotel.

The village of Llangurig lies on the banks of the Wye 4¹/₂ miles south-west of Llanidloes, just off the A470 to Rhayader. From Aberystwyth follow the A44 for about 23 miles. Bar snacks and meals, accommodation. Open 11 a.m.–2.30 p.m., 5.30–11 p.m.

The Royal Head, LLANIDLOES

(SN 954 844)

The royal head in question is that of Edward III, the victor of Crécy and Poitiers, who adorns the sign outside this seventeenth-century inn. It is his grandfather, the first Edward, who has greater relevance to Llanidloes, for he granted the lord of Powys the right to hold a weekly market here, and to defend the blossoming borough a castle and defensive earthworks were constructed. The cruciform tree-lined street system has altered little over the years, although the shops and houses have been rebuilt in later centuries. The focus of the town is the splendid half-timbered market hall of *c.* 1600, which stands right at the junction of the streets, and is the only surviving example of its kind in Wales. Elsewhere such buildings have been demolished as traffic obstacles, or rebuilt, and the fact that the Llanidloes hall has endured at all is nothing short of miraculous.

For much of its existence Llanidloes had an uneventful history, and the town only expanded beyond its medieval confines in the nineteenth century with the growth of the woollen industry. In 1839 there was a sudden uprising by workers dissatisfied with their low pay and poor living conditions. Egged on by Henry Hetherington, a founder of the Chartist movement, the mob broke into several houses and seized arms and ammunition. A large force of special policemen were drafted in to deal with the situation and some of the ringleaders were imprisoned in the Trewythen Arms, but this action only led to a violent assault on the pub and the prisoners were released. While there the mob took the opportunity of emptying the beer cellars! By contrast the history of the Royal Head is placid in the extreme, and the only event of any significance was the recent merging of the original two pubs (the King's Head and Royal Oak) into one, and the joining up of the names. There is certainly room enough for more than one pub here; the interior is spacious and falls into two halves, separated by the massive central chimney-stack. Charles I would be a more legitimate regent to occupy the sign, for the inn was probably built during his reign. The lower games room could be a later addition, but many of the original features are concealed in this part, and the timber-framed walls have been rebuilt in brick. The upper bar-lounge, however, has changed little over the centuries, apart from the removal of the timber partition wall separating the hall and inner rooms. A great stone inglenook dominates the lounge, and although a log fire no longer crackles on the hearth, the space has been utilized as a cosy seating area.

The market hall and Royal Head are among the few lucky survivors of the old town houses; Orchard House restaurant is another, and stands on the site of the castle. In 1840 Samuel Lewis wrote: 'the town has been greatly improved by the erection of several respectable buildings on the site of more ancient houses of timber frame-work . . . which formerly prevailed throughout the place'. Few urban conservationists today would agree with that statement.

The Royal Head stands in Short Bridge Street in the town centre. Llanidloes lies about 12 miles north of Rhayader on the A470 road to Newton. Bar meals, accommodation. Open 12–3 p.m., 7–11 p.m.; Saturday: 11 a.m.–11 p.m.

The Horseshoes, LLANYBLODWEL
(SJ 242 228)

Despite its Welsh name Llanyblodwel is a mile over the border in England, though for centuries the territories along the Marches were bitterly fought over by native and invader alike. Caractacus is said to have made his last stand against the Romans on nearby Llanymynech hill, and King Offa set up his great boundary dyke along the summit. In the twelfth century the Normans built Carreghofa Castle to guard the silver mines here, and to make sure the Welsh didn't stray too far from the hills. Only a few miles up river from Llanyblodwel stands the earthwork mound of Sycharth Castle, one-time home of Owain Glyndwr, who led a rebellion against the throne in 1400. But all is still here now, and the countryside is disturbed only by an occasional blast from the nearby quarries.

The Horseshoes Inn occupies a splendid site on the banks of the swift flowing Tanat, approached over an arched stone bridge. There is a large riverside car-park and beer garden, backed by the lengthy timber-framed inn, which has been made even longer by the addition of a brick and wood barn at one end. Although claimed to be fifteenth-century, the surviving details look to be at least a century later in date. This is a true village local, with several small, low-beamed rooms, and a huge stone inglenook with a real fire. There are three main ground-floor rooms, including a dining room and games room, and the bar is housed in a little turret leaning precariously out into the road. The Horseshoes was owned for generations by the Lloyd family, who brewed their own beer on site, and encouraged trade by holding a riotous festival at the inn during September, to celebrate harvest home.

The village lies just off the B4396 Llangedwyn road, about 5 miles south-west of Oswestry via the A483. Check in advance for opening times; at the time of writing the inn is due to be closed for refurbishment work.

LUDLOW

(SO 510 746)

'Ludlow was a town of coaching inns,' observed Sir Nikolaus Pevsner; and some, like the Rose and Crown off Church Street, still retain their enclosed courtyards where a coach-and-four would pull up to disgorge tired and shaken passengers, desperately in need of refreshment before the next leg of their journey. But today it is the military and ecclesiastical edifices of the Middle Ages rather than old inns and taverns which dominate the townscape and yearly attract hundreds of visitors.

This historic market town was established in the shadow of a sprawling Norman fortress – one of the earliest stone castles built in Britain – which in the fifteenth century became the seat of the Council for Wales and the

Marches. Within the Great Hall John Milton's masque *Comus* was given its first performance, in 1634, and the castle's literary association has been revived in recent years with the annual Ludlow summer festival. Peeping over the rooftops (though often invisible from street level) is the 135 ft high tower of St Lawrence's church, which contains a fine group of misericords. These wooden 'mercy rests' were used by priests to lean against, so that it looked as if they were remaining upright during the long services. Since they fulfilled such a humble function, with a less than holy part of the anatomy resting on them, it would have been ill-advised for a carver to decorate them with sacred images; and so we have a range of secular scenes depicting animals and mythological beasts, including a demon carrying off a barmaid. A sober reflection on the perils of drink perhaps, though the many taverns show that this particular lesson was never taken very seriously by the townsfolk.

Like its nearest big neighbour, Leominster, Ludlow is a bit of a maze, and Pevsner's plea that the planners should 'never decide to pull down its tortuous centre to please the gentleman motorist or the charabanc tourist' may not be echoed by every driver crawling bumper to bumper through the narrow streets. At least there is a bypass for visitors unwilling to sample Ludlow's charm by car, and the many twisting streets are best explored on foot.

Beyond the castle gates the main street broadens out to accommodate the old market-place, before narrowing in again, then widening in the region of the Bull Ring. Here cattle and sheep were penned before being taken to the market, and the inevitably named Old Bull Ring Inn is where tired farmers and drovers drank away the dust of their travels. Like many of the town houses, it is the exterior façade which really catches the eye, with half-timbering from ground to gables, and oversailing upper floors crowned with dormers. From the outside it is clear that there are really two buildings here, joined into one. It is said to date from 1365, but the rich timberwork and symmetrical façade are seventeenth century. Less obviously old is the Bull Hotel in Corve Street, where a plain eighteenth-century frontage masks an older timbered building. An oversailing first-floor veranda can be seen from the courtyard.

The *pièce-de-résistance* is the Feathers Hotel in Corve Street. 'That prodigy of timber-framed houses', as Pevsner described it, is one of the finest seventeenth-century town houses in Britain. There was reputedly an inn here as far back as 1521, but the existing structure was built in 1619 as the home of Rees Jones of Pembrokeshire, an attorney for the Council. His initials can be seen on the lock plate of the nail-studded front door. In 1670 the owners decided to make a bit of extra money by catering for travellers, and so the Feathers began its life as an inn. The first venture did not last very long, and when the Council was disbanded in 1689 the loss of trade forced the owners to close. It was not until 1752 that the house reopened for business as a coaching inn, with advertised stabling for sixty horses.

The modernized interior may come as a disappointment for the customer dazzled by the exuberantly decorated façade, and will in turn lead to the belief that only the exterior is old; but in fact many of the upper rooms retain their moulded plaster ceilings, and in one chamber there is a carved overmantel bearing the arms of James I. However, it is the façade which is the real treasure of this coaching inn, and the wealth of carvings and decorative half-timbering straddles the line between the aesthetic and the absurd. Sir Alec Clifton-Taylor's reference to another house in Ludlow as evoking 'nothing so much as a visit to the oculist' could equally be applied to the Feathers!

Ludlow is situated on the A49 between Hereford and Shrewsbury. Feathers Hotel: bar snacks and meals, accommodation. Open all day. Bull Ring Inn: bar meals. Open 11 a.m.–3 p.m, 6–11 p.m.; Friday and Saturday: 11 a.m.–11 p.m.

The Buck Inn, NEWTOWN
(SO 108 915)

Newtown was 'new' as long ago as 1279, when the surrounding territory was granted by King Edward I to the powerful Marcher lord Roger Mortimer. Roger obtained the right to hold a weekly market here, and so provided the impetus for future growth. A second period of expansion occurred with the arrival of the Montgomeryshire canal in 1819, which encouraged the development of the textile industry. Within a few years this little town on the Severn housed over fifty factories with 1,200 handlooms producing cloth and flannel by the ream. Several nineteenth-century travellers left descriptions of the industrious settlement and its environs: 'There are several woollen manufactures in and contiguous to this town, and many new dwellings; but those of tradesmen are mostly formed of wood and laths, having the intermediate parts secured with mortar or plaster, yet are warm and durable.' The streets are confined, and the houses for the most part constructed of lath and plaster.'

In more recent years Newtown has undergone yet another rebirth, as modern industrial units, factories and housing estates have sprouted up along the valley. Old buildings come down, as new ones go up. All that remains of

Newtown, the Buck Inn: a seventeenth-century lobby-entry house

the original settlement is a castle mound and the shell of St Mary's church, though many post-medieval houses survive. Most are disguised behind Georgian and Victorian façades, like the Black Boy in Broad Street; but once inside, the half-timbered panels proclaim its early origin.

There can be no mistaking the age of the Buck Inn in High Street, a black-and-white building nestling uncomfortably between indifferent brick constructions. In recent years this seventeenth-century lobby-entry house has been refurbished inside and out, but without losing any of its character or atmosphere. Most of the original features survive: the heavy oak door with its fleur-de-lis iron hinges, the timber-framed partitions separating hall from inner rooms (so often dismantled to make more space), and the chamfered ceiling beams and joists. The inglenook is particularly interesting too, since the hearth retains an early cobbled surface with the stones set on edge, the better to resist the effects of fire. From the outside the only obvious alteration to the inn has been the rendering of the ground-floor timbered walls. Less apparent on the inside is an added rear wing which contains a large dog-leg staircase rising the full height of the house. The original stair to the upper floors seems to have been in the corner next to the fireplace, where some timbers can still be seen embedded in the wall. This work was probably carried out in the eighteenth century when the owners felt the need (and had the cash) to improve and upgrade their home. The walls of the first-floor chambers were lined with elegant panels, and additional brick fireplaces built in the corners to heat up the chill rooms. Only the big ground-floor fireplace would have warmed the house before. A blocked-up door in the cellar is said to be the entrance to a passage running under the road to the site of Newtown Hall, which was demolished in 1965. Charles I is believed to have stayed overnight at the inn, though it would seem more likely that he was a guest at the Hall, where the owner was refortifying the old castle for use as a Royalist stronghold.

Newtown lies in the Severn valley between Llanidloes and Welshpool on the A483, and can be reached from Shrewsbury via the A458, or from Ludlow along the A489. Bar meals. Open 12–2.30 p.m., 5–11 p.m.

RHAYADER
(SN 970 679)

Rhayader derives its Welsh name from a series of cascades below the town, although bridge construction in 1779 reduced the torrent to a few rapids, and present-day visitors are instead drawn to the watery spectacle of the Elan Valley dams. A town of medieval origin, Rhayader was strategically important enough to receive a castle in 1177 (now vanished) and to be a frequent victim of the Norman-Welsh struggles. Even in the relatively peaceful nineteenth century the Merched Becca gangs burned the turnpike gates in protest at the extortionate tolls. From its position on the main west to east route, Rhayader was a stopping place for drovers taking their cattle from the heights of Pumlumon to the English markets, and so, consequently, had many inns and taverns catering for the wayfarers.

Some early travellers gave very different views of the place: 'a town of wretched mud hovels, invariably fronted with a pigsty, dunghill, or both . . . , or 'a stand-still little town in a remarkably pretty situation' and 'the situation of Rhayader is Romantic, its buildings are clean and neat'. Modern visitors can decide for themselves if past tourists were exaggerating or degrading the homespun comforts of mid-Wales. During the eighteenth and nineteenth centuries the main coaching inn here was the Red Lion, now no more. 'Bad' was Sir William Colt-Hoare's succinct opinion of it in 1796, but only two years later another travelogue writer, George Lipscomb, praised the hospitality and civility of the landlord, and was amazed to have a meal of roast fowl, ham, veal cutlets, cold beef, tarts and beer – all for a shilling! Even grumpy Sir William was forced to acknowledge the 'very decent accommodation' on his second visit in 1802.

The oldest pub in Rhayader is claimed to be the Triangle Inn, which is actually in the neighbouring parish of Llansantffraed Cwmdeuddwr across the river. This timber-clad pub boasts a sixteenth-century date, but was probably built a century or so later. Inside there is a stone inglenook at one end of the very low ceilinged bar. The most popular of the early pubs is the

Rhayader, the Cwmdeuddwr Arms

Cwmdeuddwr Arms in West Street. The name is Welsh for 'the valley of two waters', a reference to the meeting of the Wye and Elan just below the town. This part stone, part timbered building is typical of the older houses in the area; small, low, with thick stone walls and a large fireplace and chimney. The wood-clad front is less usual, and probably replaces wattle and daub framing. The rooms inside are not particularly spacious and can become crowded on busy days, but the pub has a wonderful farmhouse-like atmosphere. There are back-to-back inglenooks (a real log fire in the lounge), and a passage at one side leading to a pool-room in what was originally the kitchen.

Rhayader lies in the Wye valley 11 miles north-west of Builth Wells. The town is a popular tourist centre, and can be reached via the A470 from Builth or Llanidloes, or the A44 from Kington. Cwmdeuddwr: bar meals. Open 11 a.m.–11 p.m. (sometimes closed lunchtimes in winter) Triangle: bar meals. Open 11 a.m.–2.30 p.m., 6.30–11 p.m.

The Talbot, RUYTON-XI-TOWNS
(SJ 392 224)

Both names need an explanation. The eleven towns were a group of nearby settlements which merged with Ruyton in 1308 to form a small borough. A sandstone monument at one end of the town commemorates that momentous event in local history. Less ancient, but more poignant, is another memorial in the form of a cave cut into the cliff opposite the church. Inside is a carved crucifix with the names of all the local people who died in action during both World Wars. There is no real centre to Ruyton, although the focal point is the parish church with the stumpy ruins of a castle tower in the graveyard.

Of the three pubs here the timber-framed Talbot is the oldest. The sign outside depicts a sprightly talbot, an extinct breed of dog similar to a whitish bloodhound, which became the heraldic beast (and namesake) of the Talbot family. The first Earl of Shrewsbury, John Talbot, was one of the most illustrious knights of the later Middle Ages, and fought in France against Joan of Arc. It might be expected that the castle here was one of his possessions, but in fact Ruyton was held by the Earls of Arundel, and so the connection with the inn is entirely coincidental. The building dates from the seventeenth century and appears to have consisted of a hall and parlour (now the bar) separated by an entrance passage. At a later date another room was added to the hall, and a large half-timbered wing built at the rear. Recent owners have resisted the temptation to bury the interior in horse-brasses and blackened beams, and have instead opted for a more unusual style of decor. The lounge and dining room still have beamed ceilings, but the walls are papered, the lounge has an ornate Victorian fireplace, and everywhere there are shelves and shelves of old books – it looks more like a bibliophile's parlour than a pub!

Ruyton stands on the B4397 Baschurch road, 1¹/₂ miles off the A4083 Oswestry to Shrewsbury road, at Shotatton Cross. Bar snacks and meals. Open 12–3 p.m., 7–11 p.m.

SHREWSBURY
(SJ 490 125)

Like Ludlow and Leominster – the other major medieval towns on the Marches – Shrewsbury has its fair share of impressive façades and noble buildings. There are pubs aplenty for the connoisseur of taverns and good ale, and many of the buildings date back centuries. Some, like the Unicorn Inn (Wyle Cop), the Wheatsheaf (High Street) and the Old Plough (The Square), have impressive photogenic exteriors, but less distinguished interiors. In contrast, some wholly modern pub fronts conceal much older buildings, such as the Elephant and Castle (Mardol Street), with its heavy beamed ceilings. The Old Post Office Hotel, off Milk Street, has a lovely approach through a timbered gatehouse; a classic coaching inn with its own quiet, enclosed courtyard. The appearance is unfortunately spoiled by much of the 'half-timber' being nothing more than painted brickwork! Another notable inn is the String of Horses in Frankwell, a large timber-framed building constructed for a wealthy merchant in 1576. It became an inn in 1786 and was known under different names including the Royal Oak and Cross Keys, before a fire in 1912 damaged part of the ground floor. It was later reopened as a shop for the town co-operative society. However, no amount of searching will bring you to the doors of this historic hostelry, for it was dismantled in 1970 due to a road widening scheme, and later re-erected at the Avoncroft Museum of Buildings, near Bromsgrove, Worcestershire. The open-air museum also contains a splendid fifteenth-century open hall which recreates, far more accurately than any drawing, the condition of daily life in medieval buildings like the Black Swan (p. 96) and Tram Inn (p. 83).

The only town pub to live up to its venerable exterior is the King's Head in Mardol Street, a thoroughfare which retains a number of old timbered houses. The frontage is spectacular; the half-timbered façade seems to be slipping away from its neighbours as if, having stood for some 500 years, it is about to give up the ghost and nose-dive into the street. Inside the crooked and sloping ceiling furthers this impression. But no doubt the sturdy beams will hold everything in place for generations to come.

The interior has been tastefully modernized in keeping with its role as a busy town pub, but ancient wood still dominates the decor. There are no Victorian blackened timbers here, just the plain beauty of aged wood. Towards the rear there is a spacious lounge area where the bar is positioned, and in a recess to one side is the pub's secret treasure – a rare wall-painting discovered by accident in 1987 during restoration work. A team of conservationists from the University College Cardiff painstakingly uncovered and restored the painting, which has as its centre-piece the Last Supper. Though faded with age, various figures can be made out, including Jesus, Peter, and one man slipping away from the table – Judas perhaps, on his way

Shrewsbury, the fifteenth-century King's Head

to earn his thirty pieces of silver. On another part of the wall can be seen a dove carrying a wafer, which probably represents the Holy Spirit descending to Mary. Archaeologists believe the painting dates from *c.* 1500. But what are such religious motifs doing in a fifteenth-century inn? Firstly, it is not known for how long the building has been a pub, and it has only been known as the King's Head since about 1820. Before then the King's Head was the name of another establishment elsewhere in the town. Secondly, while it has undoubtedly been a domestic residence for most of its existence, the building is thought to have been associated with, or formed part of, a chapel owned by the abbot of nearby Haughmond Abbey. Earlier this century there were fourteenth-century tiles in one of the upper rooms, and these must have come from a redundant church or chapel. Perhaps at the Dissolution of the Monasteries this former ecclesiastical building was turned over to secular use.

The sign swinging outside depicts a rather haggard-looking Henry Tudor, who would have passed the inn on his way to Bosworth Field in 1485. The mayor of Shrewsbury, Thomas Mytton, had vowed to support Richard III and at first refused to allow Henry's mercenary army to cross the fortified bridge into the town. It was only to avoid the threatened destruction that Mytton relented, and opened the gates. Had he proved more stubborn, Henry would have been forced to make a lengthy, tiring detour, and the outcome at Bosworth might have been very different. To clear his conscience, Mytton lay down so that Henry could walk over him, thus absolving himself of the oath he had sworn to King Richard, that no enemy would enter the town except 'over his body'.

The historic town of Shrewsbury lies in the centre of the Marches at the junction of several major roads, including the A49 Hereford to Chester, and the A5 to Telford (M54 junction 7). Bar snacks and meals. Open 11 a.m.–11 p.m.

WELSHPOOL
(SJ 222 077)

Until the beginning of the nineteenth century this bustling border town was known simply as Pool, and the 'Welsh' prefix was added to avoid confusion with the better-known town of the same name in Dorset. Even so, Welshpool has always had the character of an English rather than a Welsh town, and as early as the 1840s travellers could write of the gas-lit streets, efficient water system, day schools, and new brick houses, in this town of 'cheerful and prepossessing appearance'. The main tourist venue here is National Trust-owned Powys Castle, which stands aloof in sumptuous gardens on the outskirts. There are several old houses that survived the various rebuilding bouts, including one with a pattern of nails on the door reading 'God damn old Oliver'; one can assume that Mr Cromwell was not universally liked hereabouts.

The oldest and most impressive of the many pubs stand almost opposite each other in Mount Street, the seventeenth-century Mermaid and Talbot. The former is by far the most striking and oft-photographed building in town, with close-set timber framing modified with usual Victorian vivacity. The lounge is small and dark, with a heavy cross-beam ceiling and a bay window overlooking the street. A side passage leading to a rear yard is a reminder of the days when any inn of some standing had to provide stabling for travellers' horses. In contrast to the black-and-white face of the Mermaid, its near neighbour, the Talbot, hides much of its half-timbering behind a rendered brick façade. Only the exposed gable wall shows any outward sign of age. Both plushly furnished lounges have beamed ceilings and cross-corner fireplaces which rise in a massive lateral chimney visible from the rear beer garden. A disused fireplace contains an interesting collection of old clay pipes.

Welshpool stands in the vale of Severn at the junction of the A483, A490 and A458, about 15 miles west of Shrewsbury. Bar meals. Open 11 a.m.–3 p.m., 7–11 p.m.

Additional inns and taverns

Bishops Castle, Boars Head (SO 324 886)
Knighton, George and Dragon, Horse and Jockey (SO 287 724)
Berriew, The Lion (SJ 187 008)
Clatter, Mytton Arms (SO 010 937)
Ellesmere, White Hart (SJ 400 347)
Glyndyfrdwy, New Inn (SJ 151 426)
Leebotwood, Pound Inn (SO 476 987)
Llanfair Waterdine, Red Lion (SO 241 763)
Picklescott, Bottle and Glass (SO 435 995)
Sellatyn, Cross Keys (SJ 267 340)
Trefeglwys, Red Lion (SN 970 906)

5. CHESTER AND NORTH-EAST WALES

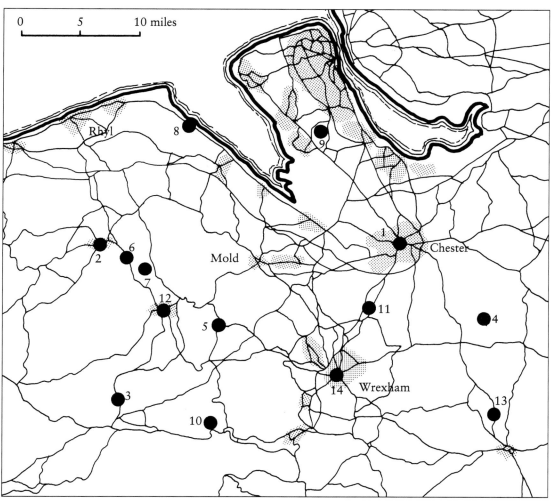

0   5   10 miles

Rhyl

8

9

2   6
7
12
Mold
5

1
Chester
11
4

3
10
14   Wrexham
13

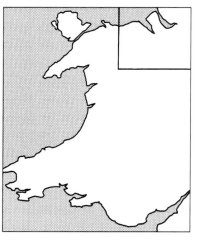

1. Chester
2. Denbigh
3. Gwyddelwern
4. Higher Burwardsley
5. Llanarmon
6. Llanrhaeadr
7. Llanynys
8. Mostyn
9. Raby
10. Rhewl
11. Rossett
12. Ruthin
13. Tushingham
14. Wrexham

CHESTER

(SJ 405 660)

The hand of the Victorian restorer is everywhere evident in this most popular and photogenic of British cities. Few early buildings have escaped being thoroughly renovated and having their timbers blackened with pitch, and panels gleamingly whitewashed – the indelible image of what we call half-timbering today. Some of the houses have been reconstructed, others built from scratch in an antiquated style; all add to the magnificent confusion of architectural styles on display at modern Chester. Here and there are fragments of columns, excavated buildings and sunken foundations which reveal the Roman origin of the city, and the rigid street system of the imperial fortress dictated the layout of the Saxon and later settlements on the site. Most famous of all are the unique 'Rows', a series of covered walkways built out over ground-floor shops.

Even though many of the city buildings have been modernized beyond recognition, some of the road-level shops retain very early features, such as the splendid medieval vaulted cellar in the Old Crypt wine bar (Watergate Street). There are dozens of inns and taverns in the city, and while many are centuries old, their ancient features are usually hidden behind more recent façades. The plain rendered walls of the Blue Bell wine bar (Northgate Street) conceals an attractive half-timbered front with diagonally arranged panels. The first-floor restaurant nestles under a splendid fifteenth-century open timber roof.

At Row level in Eastgate Street is the more obviously old Boot Inn, dated 1643, its well-restored timbered front complete with busty nymphs propping up the beams. The interior is long and low with split-level bars, and careful restoration has returned the beamed ceiling to its original, unblackened state. Of all the timber-framed buildings in Chester, few can compete with the Bear and Billet in Lower Bridge Street. There are over 1,600 panes of glass in the elaborate, four-storey façade, the windows supported on rows of richly carved brackets. The Bear was built in 1664 as a town house of the Earls of Shrewsbury, though the sign depicts the bear and ragged staff badge of the Earls of Warwick. It is said to have replaced a building destroyed in the Civil War, when Royalist Chester was besieged by Roundhead troops.

A little further along Bridge Street is another pub with Civil War connections. The Old King's Head has a sign depicting Charles I, who stayed in Chester in 1645, and from the battlements saw the defeat of his army at nearby Rowton Moor. The king then fled down Bridge Street and crossed the

Chester, the Bear and Billet

Chester, the Old King's Head

Dee into Wales. The pub was already standing then, having been built around 1633, though it is doubtful that Charles popped in for a quick drink. Like the Bear, this pub was originally a dwelling house, with some rooms later put aside for commercial use. It was built for the mayor of Chester, Randle Holme, whose descendants were famous heralds and historians of the county. Only the oversailing top floors retain their half-timbered panels, and the remaining walls have been rebuilt in more durable materials. The interior is surprisingly spacious, with comfortable seats along the walls, and stools and tables arranged around the tree-like pillars which support the beamed ceiling. An adjacent house has been incorporated into the premises as a separate dining room and restaurant.

Pride of place among the city pubs must be reserved for the Falcon, a handsome and complex building which stands at the corner of Grosvenor and Bridge Streets. This has long been identified as a seventeenth-century house built over medieval cellars, but careful restoration work in 1982 proved that the building was not all that it appeared to be. What started life as a town house became an inn from 1778 until 1878, and was then used as a textile factory, an office and finally a store. The empty and dilapidated building was in dire need of repair work, and any decayed beams were replaced or supported by new timbers in such a way as not to spoil the character of the interior. During the course of the work it became clear that the house was not all of one build; the present lounge is separated from the bar by a timbered partition in which can be seen a large Tudor doorway and an unglazed window – but what is a window doing inside a house? The reason is that the front of the building incorporates a former Row, and both door and window would have opened on to a raised walkway in front of the house. The upper floor was carried over the Row and supported on a series of carved timber posts.

Records suggest that a property here was acquired by Sir Richard Grosvenor around 1602, though Pevsner dated the building to 1626, and other documents indicate that the Grosvenor family built the house around 1640. However, there can be little doubt that most of the Falcon as it now stands was built in the early years of the seventeenth century on the remains of a medieval house. On the side facing the Row there were two chambers – shops or workrooms – separated by a passageway which led to the rear wing. This would have been the private quarters of the family, but is now a separate bar and dining room, with a large stone fireplace and a timber mullioned window which has been pushed out of shape by the weight of the beams. A few decades after the house was built the Grosvenor family, among the other residents of the city, were caught up in the bitter struggle between king and parliament. Chester was fortified and held for the king, and Richard Grosvenor was employed in the garrison. He later petitioned the mayor and city assembly to be allowed to incorporate the Row into his house, since the premises were too small for his family. This seems rather unlikely considering the size of the building (though admittedly we do not know the size of his family), but the mayor seems to have been swayed by the fact that Richard was helping to defend the city. He agreed to his request, on payment of an annual rent of 2s 6d.

On a historical note it is curious to learn that in 1540 a law was passed forbidding 'any woman between 14 and 40 years of age' from keeping a tavern or alehouse in the city 'under pain of 40 shillings forfeiture'. There seems to have been an unfair and deep-rooted mistrust of landladies in Chester, and in the medieval miracle plays one of the condemned souls in hell is an unscrupulous ale wife: 'Deceaving many a creature, with hoppes I made my ale stronge, Ashes and erbes I blende amonge, and marred so good maulte.' Even George Borrow was told an awful (and no doubt untrue) rhyme on his visit here in 1862:

> Chester ale, Chester ale, I could ne'er get it down,
> 'Tis made of ground-ivy, of dirt, and of bran,
> 'Tis as thick as a river below a huge town!
> 'Tis not lap for a dog, far less drink for a man.

The city of Chester stands on the banks of the Dee, between Ellesmere Port and Wrexham, M56 junction 15. Access from Wales via A55 and A483. Old Boot Inn: bar meals. Open 11 a.m.–3.30 p.m., 5.30–11 pm.; Friday and Saturday: 11 a.m.–11 p.m. King's Head and Falcon: bar snacks and meals. Open 11 a.m.–11 p. m.

The Golden Lion, DENBIGH
(SJ 051 661)

Denbigh, like nearby Ruthin (p. 154), was a fortified town established in the aftermath of a Welsh uprising in 1282. A large castle was built on the summit of a hill to protect the settlement and defend the surrounding area, but today, some seven centuries later, the old centre is virtually uninhabited, and modern Denbigh has grown up around the lower slopes of the hill. John Leland commented: 'I have not yet lernid the certente how this wallid toune decayed . . . wither it were by fier or for lak of water;' but it may be that the townsfolk were simply fed up with the steep and windy site. Within a few years of Leland's visit the Earl of Leicester tried to boost the prestige of Denbigh by building a grand new church within the old town, which was probably meant to replace St Asaph cathedral. But although the earl's venture ended in ruin like the castle, the town thrived and grew.

In the vicinity of the market square new buildings were constructed in the sixteenth and seventeenth centuries, and one of the earliest which still survives is the Golden Lion in Back Row. All trace of the external timberwork has been hidden behind a thick coat of cement, but the overhanging upper floor and Tudor-arch door are giveaways. Inside, the lounge and bar are separated by a fine post-and-panel partition which is still largely intact. The interior layout has changed little over the centuries, and it is still possible to make out the small rooms at the front where the occupants carried out their business. The

A street scene in early seventeenth-century Denbigh, showing the likely original appearance of the Golden Lion

larger rooms at the rear were used as living quarters. The rear hall has been turned into a lounge extension, and the architectural details suggest it is a seventeenth-century addition to the sixteenth-century front wing. On the walls are old photographs and etchings of the various ancient monuments in Denbigh – the castle, Leicester's church, the Goblin tower, the Carmelite friary – and a more incongruous touch is provided by a collection of ceramic pigs!

The pub is unobtrusively located behind a row of shops in a popular area for inns and taverns. There is another Lion next door, and a few yards away is the much older Eagles, a lobby-entry house dated 1643. The main coaching inn of the town was the Bull Hotel, behind the sixteenth-century market hall (which contains an excellent display on the history of Denbigh). The Bull is said to date from 1666, but has been thoroughly refurbished in later years, and the fake half-timbering and tile-hung front belong to a face-lift of *c.* 1900. Sir William Colt-Hoare stayed here in 1801 and pronounced it 'an old-fashioned house and as old-fashioned a landlady'. The great oak staircase rises to the full height of the building, and near the top the outlines of hands have been carved into the wood. Are they a reference to the town's former glove trade, or the 'hand' crest of the wealthy Myddletons of Chirk Castle?

Denbigh town lies in the Vale of Clwyd 9 miles south of Rhyl along the A525. Bar snacks. Open 11 a.m.–11 p.m.

The Rose and Crown, GWYDDELWERN
(SJ 075 467)

When the Revd Mr Warner passed through the Dee valley in 1797, he was startled by a 'fierce gigantic figure' painted over the door of the Owain Glyndwr Inn at Corwen. That image of the fifteenth-century warrior is still preserved today, and serves to remind travellers that they are in the heart of the officially designated 'Glyndwr district'. A few miles away at Glyndyfrdwy is a prominent castle mound graced with Owain's name, from where his army is believed to have marched away to sack Ruthin on the first day of the uprising, in September 1400. The easiest route from the vale of Dee to the vale of Clwyd was past Gwyddelwern church, where an inn would have been ideally sited to catch passing trade. The Rose and Crown was not standing then, so we can forget the appealing image of Owain's small army staggering out of the pub in the direction of Ruthin, fired up with ale and enthusiasm. Another hundred years or more were to pass before a carpenter's gang raised the first timbers of the pub in place.

Apart from the church, the village has no other antiquities to capture the attention of passing tourists, and so there are no early references to the Rose and Crown. When Sir William Colt-Hoare stopped here in 1801, he left the coach driver to freshen up (at the inn?) while taking a stroll around St Beuno's church. Did the eminent antiquarian choose not to pay much attention to the inn, or had it by then assumed the disguise it now wears? From the outside the plain rendered walls conceal all signs of age, only the irregularly spaced windows and massive central chimney-stack hinting that the building is older than it looks. But inside all is revealed; the lounge and pool-room have heavy cross-beamed ceilings, and a disused inglenook so large that it now accommodates part of the bar. Behind a rare, almost intact post-and-panel partition is another lounge and dining area, which has been extended in more recent times.

In the private rooms on the first floor some of the decorative roof trusses are visible; others are boxed in by inserted ceilings, but they were originally meant to be seen. The Rose and Crown is a timber-framed house dating from the early sixteenth century, and may have evolved from an open hall like the Tram Inn (p. ??), although many changes over the years have obscured the original layout. The timber framing has been hidden beneath drab rendering, depriving the building of its former splendour. From the inside it is clear that the gable walls were elaborately decorated with timbers set in diamond and chevron patterns, though oddly the pattern is not symmetrical. It is difficult to see why the carpenter made such a blunder (if mistake it was), and there are other oddities here too. A number of ceiling beams have been chamfered on one side only, and for some reason the craftsman never finished carving all the stops on the joists. Did the owners run out of money, or did some other reason prevent them from adding the finishing touches to their fine new home four centuries ago?

Gwyddelwern lies on the A494 Ruthin to Bala road, about 2 miles north of Corwen. Bar meals. Open 12–3 p.m. (Saturday and Sunday), 7–11p.m.

The Pheasant, HIGHER BURWARDSLEY
(SJ 524 566)

Pick a fine, clear day to visit the Pheasant, for the views are spectacular. Sited on a chain of sandstone hills which culminate in the castle-crowned peak of Beeston, the inn enjoys unparalleled views across the Cheshire plain to the Mersey, west to the Welsh mountains, and as far east as the hazy Peak District. The proprietors have exploited this breathtaking vista to the full, restoring the dilapidated farm buildings, building a patio area and water garden, and adding tasteful modern extensions with large windows. The Pheasant has come a long way from its simple beginnings as a farm-cum-inn, as an old photograph in the lounge shows. There is the main building itself (then known as the Carden Arms) with its sandstone lower half and timbered upper, a small cluster of outbuildings (now either gone or renovated as guest rooms), and a small copse of trees to shelter the farmstead from the worst of the winter storms. Whether through decay, or the need to improve the view, the trees have gone and their place has been taken by a less welcome row of telegraph poles.

Customers impressed by either the view or the landlord's prize-winning herd of Highland cattle, should spare more than a glance at the building itself. It was constructed probably in the early seventeenth century to a simple rectangular plan of two rooms, the larger being the hall. There is an adjoining kitchen wing, but this could be a later addition. The old hall is now a residents' lounge, with elegant wainscoting lining the inglenook, behind which is another fireplace with ovens serving the kitchen. Since the main fireplace is positioned in the side wall, this places the Pheasant in the 'lateral chimney' group of houses, a group which often includes dwellings of a higher social and architectural standing. Huge ceiling beams on the first floor can almost decapitate unwary guests.

The lower bar has been largely rebuilt in stone, but the half-timbered partition dividing up the room is the outer wall of the original house. Look out for carpenters' marks on the jointed timbers. In a cage by the window sits a green parrot that occasionally says hello to customers; but at the time of my visit it was as motionless as the stuffed pheasant over the fireplace.

Higher Burwardsley lies about 8 miles south-east of Chester, and can be reached via several signposted country lanes off the A41 and A534. Perhaps the best way is from Chester to Whitchurch along the A41, and turn off at Milton Green for Tattenhall village. Pass through the village and follow the signs for Burwardsley; just after the first group of houses are passed, a left fork leads up the hillside to Higher Burwardsley. Bar snacks and meals, accommodation. Open 11 a.m.–3 p.m., 7–11 p.m.

The Raven, LLANARMON-YN-IAL
(SJ 190 562)

Llanarmon lies in the limestone belt of the Vale of Clwyd, and everywhere there are steep and narrow rocky valleys, old mines, quarries and caves. The ground is so tough that King John had to order mallets for the workmen to break the stones in the ditch of his castle here. On the hillside across from the rocky castle mound stands the large parish church of St Harmon and, beside the graveyard, the imposing Raven Inn. A datestone set in the end wall records the building of the inn in 1722, although it has been extended and modernized since then. It is basically two buildings joined end to end, and the division is clear when seen from the large beer garden in front. Inside there are two separate lounges (one of which closes if customers are few) with large inglenook fireplaces and beamed ceilings. While in the village call into the church to see the fourteenth-century carved tombstone of Gruffudd ap Llywelyn, which is said to have been brought from Valle Crucis Abbey near Llangollen. According to a blackly humorous story the knight was killed fighting in the Holy Land when a sword stroke disembowelled him, and a dog ran away with his guts. The little miscreant can be seen at the feet of the effigy.

Llanarmon-yn-Ial can be reached by following the B5430 for about 2 miles, from where it leaves the main A494 Ruthin to Mold road. Alternatively follow the B5431 at a signposted junction on the A525 Ruthin to Wrexham road. Bar meals. Open 12–3 p.m., 6.30–11 p.m.

The King's Head, LLANRHAEADR
(SJ 082 633)

The King's Head is one of those rarities, a centuries-old pub which has been completely refurbished to modern standards, but without losing too many of the original features. It is also unusual to find a country pub which stays open all day! The interior is a warren of small, thick-walled rooms and passages with low, beamed ceilings of polished wood. The original seventeenth-century lobby-entry house has been greatly extended at the back, and the old hall converted into the 'Witch and Warlock' bar (though there seems to be no story behind this). The temptation to strip the walls to the bare stone has been avoided, and the whitewashed walls lighten up the interior immensely – very necessary too, for the inn is located in a hollow below the church, and the wheels of vehicles travelling along the A525 speed past the windows. The old road through the village once forded the stream beside the inn, and then climbed the steep hillside past the blacksmith's shop. Locals remember that the road was so steep that spare horses were kept at the smithy to help pull coaches. Such an obstacle was no problem to modern-day planners, and the incline was flattened out – hence the sunken look of the inn. Even the front door had to be moved round to the back!

No one should leave Llanrhaeadr without having visited the church of St Dyfnog to see the magnificent Jesse window. The early sixteenth-century stained glass depicts the genealogy of Christ in the form of a family tree growing out of the body of his ancestor, Jesse. King David, Solomon, and the prophets Isaiah and Moses are shown, dressed in medieval costume as was the convention of the time. Nearby is a pompous Baroque effigy of Maurice Jones (d. 1702), a 'Gentleman of Fine Parts of Body and Mind' we are informed. Plump cherubs weep by his side. Finally, hunt down St Dyfnog's holy well which lies beyond the churchyard, where the stream gushes out of the hillside and fills a baptistry. This is, presumably, the insignificant 'rhaeadr' or waterfall after which the village is named.

The village of Llanrhaeadr lies just off the A525 midway between Ruthin and Denbigh in the Vale of Clwyd. Bar snacks and meals. Open 11 a.m.–11 p.m.

Cerrigllwydion Arms, LLANYNYS
(SJ 103 627)

Llanynys, the 'church in the meadows', is an ancient Celtic foundation lying in the fertile farmlands of the Vale of Clwyd. The meandering ribbons of the Clywedog and Clwyd rivers are prone to flooding, and it is said that parishioners would sometimes arrive for services at the church by boat! It may well have been with this in mind that an unknown medieval craftsman painted the figure of St Christopher on the nave wall; the image of the saint carrying the Christ child through the flood was something damp-footed worshippers could identify with. Llanynys church also contains rare wooden dog tongs, which the churchwardens purchased for 2*s*. 6*d* in 1757. The implement was used to drag stray dogs off the premises, and there is a story that during one canine fracas the vicar halted the service to cheer his dog on!

The Cerrigllwydion Arms stands next to the church gate, and was built partly inside the graveyard at the insistence of the vicar, who did not want the pub to block his view of Denbigh Castle. It is said to date from the fourteenth century, but this is a rather over-optimistic estimate, and despite the bare stone walls and blackened beams the building does not appear to be older than the eighteenth century. The bar and upper lounge occupy the earliest surviving parts of the building, each room having a large stone fireplace and a beamed ceiling festooned with jugs and glittering brassware. Several old photographs and sketches show how the pub looked in days gone by. Over the years this simple lobby-entry house has been greatly extended and the most recent addition is a lovely half-timbered dining room with views across the Vale of Clwyd. Sitting here, one can sympathize with the aesthetically-minded vicar.

Llanynys lies midway between Ruthin and Denbigh, and can best be reached along signposted country lanes from either Pentre, or Rhewl, villages, off the A525. Alternatively the pub can be reached from the B5429 between Llanbedr-dyffryn-Clwyd and Bodfari. Bar snacks and meals. Open 11.30 a.m.–3 p.m., 7–11 p.m. (closed Monday lunchtimes); Sunday: 12–3 p.m., 7–10.30 p.m.

Hen Dafarn and Lletty Hotel, MOSTYN
(SJ 177 791, AND SJ 157 807)

Though only built a few generations apart, these two Deeside pubs could hardly be more different in appearance. The Lletty is a tall, imposing building, well proportioned, with rows of sash windows, neatly chamfered beams, and huge stone fireplaces at either end of the building; a classic coaching inn of the late seventeenth century. By contrast, Hen Dafarn is a low, thatched cottage of little, if any, architectural finesse, which epitomizes the insubstantial dwellings most poor Welsh farmers lived in. There is a large stone fireplace at one end, with the date 1664 carved into the beam. A second fireplace half-way along the building has gone, although the top of its chimney still pokes through the thatch! Hen Dafarn was originally a late medieval cruck hall, but only three of the plain, tapering trusses now remain. The cutaway drawing shows how the building would have appeared in 1664 when the half-timbered walls had been rebuilt in stone, and the open hearth replaced with a cleaner and safer stone chimney. Unlike many other converted halls, Hen Dafarn did not have an upper floor inserted into the roof space, but additional room was provided by a two-storeyed wing later built at one end, and this now forms the bar.

Just over a mile further along the road to Prestatyn is the Lletty Hotel, tucked away beneath a steep wooded hillside. Until a few years ago this was known as Lletty Gonest, the Honest Man inn, and a gaudily painted bust of the eponymous gent stares out at the customer from the stonework over the entrance. He has a lamb slung over his shoulder, recalling his failed trade as a butcher, and beneath the effigy is the date 1699. There is a story that the

Honest Man came from Worcestershire searching for a suitable place to build an inn, and eventually settled here on the coast. The financial costs proved a heavy burden, but he paid off all his creditors (gaining the enviable sobriquet), fitted out the inn for business, and then disappeared. Today the inn is a much more spacious building than it was 300 years ago, for the central corridor which led to the rear stairs has gone, and the two ground-floor rooms have been thrown into one. There is a pool room at one end housed in a later extension. Only one of the gable fireplaces now remains, since the other chimney collapsed when the adjoining boiler house was removed. A painting in the elegant wood-panelled lounge shows the inn as it appeared before that unfortunate mishap.

Behind the panelling is a secret passage leading to a blocked well, which is said to connect with a cave on the sea front. This legend probably arose on account of the smugglers who used the inn as a base for their nefarious activities. These were no rough thugs scavenging the wrecks along the estuary, but a professional group of well-to-do criminals. In the early eighteenth century a group of custom officials surprised a gang of colliers unloading barrels of port wine. In the ensuing fight the officers realized that the men were wearing rings and had fine clothes under their scruffy overalls – not that the revelation proved anything in the end, for they were trussed up and left on the shore while the gang made off with their booty. Needless to say, they were never caught.

Hen Dafarn and Lletty Hotel are roadside pubs on the A548 between Flint and Prestatyn. Opening times at Hen Dafarn are irregular and restricted to evenings. Lletty: Bar snacks and meals, accommodation. Open 11.30 a.m.–11 p.m. (Monday to Saturday).

The Wheatsheaf, RABY
(SJ 312 798)

The small Wirral village of Raby lies only a short distance from the busy Chester to Birkenhead road, yet it remains aloof and remote, unalterably rural. Even the plain, half-timbered exterior of this thatched inn furthers the impression, and the car-park is in a farmyard! Around thirty years ago it was described in a local guidebook as 'a rather rough, bare interior with wooden benches and a deep inglenook, and beer served in blue banded mugs'. Today, however, the Wheatsheaf is surprisingly modern, and very popular with homeward bound commuters. This is a long, low, whitewashed building which still retains some timber framing, though most of the walls have been rebuilt in brick and stone. Over the front door is a brick inscribed with the date 1611 which may record the construction of the inn, but since it is set into the later stonework it cannot be an original feature. Inside, the oldest part of the building is the central bar-lounge with a flagstone floor and rough-hewn beamed ceiling. Recent extensions at either end of the pub harmonize with the older parts, but the main attention-grabber here is the huge central inglenook – still impressive despite the inserted brick arches and hearth.

The Wheatsheaf lies just south of Raby village, off the A540 Heswall road. Alternatively, leave the M53 at junction 4, and follow the B5151 towards Willaston until a signposted right turn leads to Raby. Bar meals (lunchtimes only). Open: 11.30 a.m.–3 p.m., 5.30–10.30 p.m.; Sunday: 12–2 p.m., 7–10.30 p.m.

The Sun Inn, RHEWL
(SJ 177 447)

High up on the Dee valley stands the Sun Inn, a solid whitewashed stone building, looking like the last outpost of civilization before the heights of Llantysilio mountain are reached. For the drovers and shepherds descending the gorse- and heather-clad hills, the inn would have been a most welcome haven, and even today, some two centuries or more since it was built, the Sun retains a marvellously cosy farmhouse atmosphere. There are two large inglenooks in a huge projecting chimney-stack, and the fireplace in the narrow rear room probably served a kitchen – the remains of an oven recess can be seen beneath the curving oak lintel. On the walls of the lounge are framed antiquarian prints of local tourist haunts including the Pontcysyllte aqueduct, Castell Dinas Bran, and Valle Crucis Abbey. In the bar the decor takes a less usual turn with coal-mining mementos, but then the choice of Felinfoel beer on tap is unusual too, since the brewery is in distant Llanelli.

From Llangollen town follow the A542 Ruthin road for about a mile to where a signposted left turn leads to Llandynam and Rhewl. The inn lies beyond the village, about 1½ miles from the turn. A more scenic but twisting route can be followed from Glyndyfrdwy on the Llangollen-Corwen road. Bar meals. Open 12–3 p.m., 7–11 p.m.

The Golden Grove, ROSSETT

(SJ 354 586)

The Golden Grove at Rossett is not one of the easiest pubs to find, but a visit is well worth the effort. In fact it is some distance from the village of Rossett, down a country lane signposted to Llyndir Hall, and stands in what appears at first glance to be a village of half-timbered houses. The original part of the inn was a fairly modest cottage of late sixteenth- or early seventeenth-century date, but over the years it has spawned a large family of look-alikes, though some, unfortunately, do not look very genuine at all. A sign reading 'This is the Golden Grove' greets you as you enter, but on an early nineteenth-century map it is marked simply as Grove. Perhaps the 'Golden' was added to reflect the numerous discoveries of Roman coins made in the vicinity over the years. The village of Rossett stands on, or near, the line of a road from the mine workings at Minera to the legionary fortress at Chester. Several of the coins are displayed behind the bar, which certainly makes a change from the usual horse-brass decor. But the Golden Grove is unusual in another respect: what other pub can boast a tombstone in the dining room?

Although unknown to many customers at the bar, this incongruous slab is an uncomfortable reminder of mortality for those dining around it. But what is it doing inside a building? The reason is simple enough; the room was built over what was once an open field at the rear of the pub, but still leaves the question of why there should be a grave in someone's backyard! The inscription commemorates James Clark who died, aged sixty, on 20 April 1880. Mr Clark, it would seem, was a con-man, putting on airs and graces, living the life of a country squire, but without much money in his pocket. His roving eye alighted on the delectable landlady of the Golden Grove, and before long his glib tongue had managed to convince her to give him board and lodging in return for all his worldly wealth when he died. When the time came for Mr Clark to shuffle off this mortal coil, the poor woman was horrified to learn that he was penniless, and in revenge buried him with every expense spared, in the back garden! This, at least, is the story told, though the stone also carries the line 'in affectionate remembrance', so perhaps the landlady was not as heartless and vengeful as the tale suggests.

Less obvious than a 3 ft high chunk of stone, but no less interesting, is a group of delicately carved wooden figures fixed to the beams around the lounge. They originally graced a huge Welsh dresser which was unfortunately too decayed to save in its entirety. Note too, a tiny square window cut into the end wall of the cavernous inglenook. It faces the front door because, according to local folklore, witches and demons would not enter a house if they could see the welcoming glow of a fire from the threshold.

Today customers can enjoy a quiet pint at the Grove any time of the week (provided the pub is open), but generations ago the licensing laws were more restrictive and anyone caught drinking on a Sabbath would be fined. 'The district is infested with Sunday drinkers,' screamed the local newspapers, although the police found it difficult to gather evidence against the culprits since there were plenty of thirsty locals willing to act as look-outs. The trick was for the landlord to place a flagon of beer or ale on the bar, which was drunk by the customer, who left a 'donation' upon leaving!

The Golden Grove lies just over a mile north-west of Rosset village, near the hamlet of Burton Green, and can be reached along a signposted country lane from the Rosset to Chester road. Bar snacks and meals. Open 11.30 a.m.–11 p.m.

The Star, RUTHIN
(SJ 123 582)

'This ancient town is fast losing its antique appearance,' bemoaned a contributor to *Archaeologia Cambrensis* in 1870. 'It contained, a short time ago a number of houses, in the walls of which black beams of timber were conspicuous, which caused the observer to ruminate on the good old days of Queen Elizabeth.' One wonders if a Catholic martyr would have agreed with that Victorian ruminator. A more recent loss was the Ship Inn, a timber-framed fifteenth-century cruck hall, demolished in 1965 to allow road widening. Though much has already gone, Ruthin has not suffered the extensive and thoughtless rebuilding inflicted on many other old towns. There is still a wealth of historic buildings here, such as the thirteenth-century castle, vandalized by Cromwell's soldiers, and rebuilt in the last century as a hotel. Timber-framed Exmewe Hall was the sixteenth-century home of the Lord Mayor of London, though it was reconstructed in 1928 and is now a bank. On the large block of stone outside, King Arthur is said to have beheaded one of his rivals in a love affair. The nearby court-house dates from the fifteenth century and is also a bank; the stump of a gibbet protrudes from the west gable. At least the medieval mill off Clwyd Street has nothing remotely morbid connected with it.

Several of Ruthin's pubs are several hundred years old, but have been extensively modernized. The cellars of the Wine Vaults in St Peter's Square are said to be medieval, though everything above them certainly is not. More impressive is the Wynnstay Hotel, which is half-timbered in part, and has a long, sweeping tiled roof sprinkled with dormer windows. On the steep road down from the market square to the old mill stands a much less obtrusive building, the Star. Indeed, few travellers may spare the pub more than a passing glance; but what a difference it would make if the plain rendered walls were stripped away to reveal the half-timbered building underneath. This is a small and compact lobby-entry house reputedly built in the twelfth century, but a more probable date is *c.* 1600. The oldest part is the front block facing the road, which now houses the bar and lounge and contains a central stone chimney with back-to-back fireplaces. Both fireplaces have been modernized, but all the old beams remain intact, and the ceiling is strikingly painted red and black. The rear stone hall was added some years later, and one of the beams upstairs is said to be inscribed with the date 1639. The far end of the ground-floor room is dominated by a splendid sooty inglenook, with a recess at one side in which a blocked opening can be seen. This looks like an old window, but the landlord recalls a story that the opening formed part of a secret passage leading to the castle on the hill above.

Ruthin is situated in the Vale of Clwyd, 6 miles south-east of Denbigh along the A525, and 10 miles south-west of Mold. The Star lies in Clwyd Street, west of the town square. Bar meals. Open 11 a.m.–11 p.m.; Sunday: 12–3 p.m., 7–11 p.m. Closed lunchtimes in winter.

The Blue Bell, TUSHINGHAM
(SJ 523 454)

This superb old coaching inn stands on the main road from Whitchurch to Chester, in the tiny village of Bell o' th' Hill, more properly part of Tushingham. There is only a scatter of farms here, served by two parish churches though the older, St Chad's, is now a forlorn edifice mouldering in a meadow some distance from the road. Only summer services and funerals are conducted there. Still the seventeenth-century brick building continues to play a dark role in folklore of the area. It is said that owls fly from the tower at midnight and circle around the home of someone who is about to die. A little more cheery (though no less morbid) is the story told of the bizarre ghost which once haunted the inn. One of the previous landlords kept a pet duck in the bar, but as it grew from a cuddly ball of down into a fully feathered monster, it took to viciously pecking customers' ankles. Eventually the landlord resorted to 'fowl' play, but not having the heart to cook the duck for supper, he buried its carcase under the bottom step of the cellar stair. But murder will out, and soon customers complained of sharp pecks to their legs and began to glimpse feathery spectres. So the desperate landlord employed the help of no less than twelve parsons to exorcize the deceased duck, but instead of vanishing the ghost began to shrink until it was small enough for a

Tushingham, the Blue Bell: this cutaway view shows the developing trends of the Renaissance house. Although built to a lobby-entry plan, the central stair allowed better circulation and greater privacy. The main building appears to be an extension of 1667 to the older house on the right

quick-thinking parson to slip it in a bottle and cork it. To be extra sure no one would open the bottle in future, it was sealed up in a wall cavity and, so we may assume, is there to this day.

Strangely enough, during recent renovations to the inn a 400-year-old mummified rat was found entombed in the wall. This is the most gruesome of the many objects found on the premises by the owners, and is now on display in the bar; other finds include crockery, coins, a Cavalier's hat and a pair of ladies' shoes – the height of fashion in 1735!

Over the front door there is an inscription recording the construction of the Blue Bell in 1667, although the door itself has been moved from its original position. On display in the dining room is a photograph taken around 1900 which shows that the existing porch was formerly open sided, with the little first-floor chamber supported on carved posts. Inside there is a lobby with a timber stair leading to the upper chambers, and large rooms on either side of the central chimney-stack. The bar is housed in the main hall, with its massive beamed ceiling and cavernous inglenook. There is said to be a blocked priest's hole at the back of the fireplace. Low doors beyond the hall lead into a separate wing with its own fireplace and stair, and which now contains two comfortable dining rooms on the ground floor. The loftier chambers above have open roofs with curving timbers sweeping up to meet the rafters. Such an early feature points to this wing being the original house, rather than an extension added after 1667. It may be that the family, having lived in the smaller, more cramped house for generations, required the space (and prestige) of a grander house; and instead of demolishing the older dwelling once the new one was built, kept it as extra living space, or as accommodation for guests staying at the inn. The fine carvings on the porch and around the early windows testify to the pride the long-departed owners had for their new dwelling, and their understandable desire to impress the neighbours.

The Blue Bell lies just off the A41, about 2¹/₂ miles north-west of Whitchurch. Bar snacks and meals. Open 12–3 p.m., 6–11 p.m.

The Horse and Jockey, WREXHAM
(SJ 334 503)

The elaborate Perpendicular tower of St Giles's church is said to be one of the seven wonders of Wales, though perhaps an even greater wonder is that the

Horse and Jockey has managed to survive the wholesale rebuilding of the town centre since the last war. Such thatched buildings were once a common sight in Wrexham, but today the pub looks quite out of place; a forlorn, incongruous relic. When Dr Johnson visited the town he considered the houses to be 'highly commendable', and photographs in W.A. William's book *Old Wrexham* (1983) shows how many fine buildings have been lost over the years. An early casualty was the timber-framed Hand Inn (demolished 1899), with oversailing dormers reminiscent of the King's Head, Chester (p. 141). The Talbot went in 1904, a long, low seventeenth-century building which was once the meeting place of the first nonconformist community in Wrexham. So we should at least be grateful that the Horse and Jockey is still with us.

The pub has been restored on a number of occasions, and the interior strikes the right balance between the old and new. There are two main bars, and a long rear restaurant under a superb open roof. The few remaining scraps of ancient timbers are preserved in brickwork like precious fossils. This was originally a half-timbered building, although virtually all the walls have been rebuilt in brick or stone over the years. High up in the narrow passage between the restaurant and lounge can be seen part of the original gable which escaped rebuilding; there is an unglazed window which would have looked out over the yard, but was blocked when the rear wing was built. During the nineteenth century this wing was a pub known as the Colliers, while the older front part was used as cottages. In 1868 both parts were merged, and in 1886 the pub was renamed the Horse and Jockey, in memory of champion jockey Fred Archer who died at the tender age of twenty-nine. The sign outside was painted with a likeness of Fred, although the existing portrait is a 1938 copy. The oldest part of the building is the lounge-bar facing the main street, which was originally two separate rooms heated by large cross-corner fireplaces. All the details suggest a seventeenth century date, but one local historian has pointed out that the pub does not appear on a town map of 1790!

Located in Hope Street in Wrexham town centre. Wrexham lies off the A488 between Chester and Oswestry. Bar snacks and meals. Open: 11 a.m.–6 p.m., 7–11 p.m.; Sunday: 12–3 p.m., 7–10.30 p.m.

Additional inns and taverns

Abergele, The Harp (SH 945 775)

Barton, Cock o' Barton (SJ 447 541)

Capel Garmon, White Horse (SH 816 554)

Caergwrle, Old Castle Inn (SJ 304 574)

Connah's Quay, Gawain and the Green Knight (SJ 283 700)

Cilcain, White Horse (SJ 177 653)

Dyserth, New Inn (SJ 055 793)

Erbistock, Boat Inn (SJ 354 413)

Ewloe, Boar's Head (SJ 296 667)

Halkyn, Britannia (SJ 210 710)

Isycoed, Plough Inn (SJ 405 501)

Llanfwrog, Cross Keys (SJ 113 577)

Maeshafn, Loggerheads Inn (SJ 198 625)

Pontblyddyn, Bridge Inn (SJ 277 604)

6. NORTH-WEST WALES

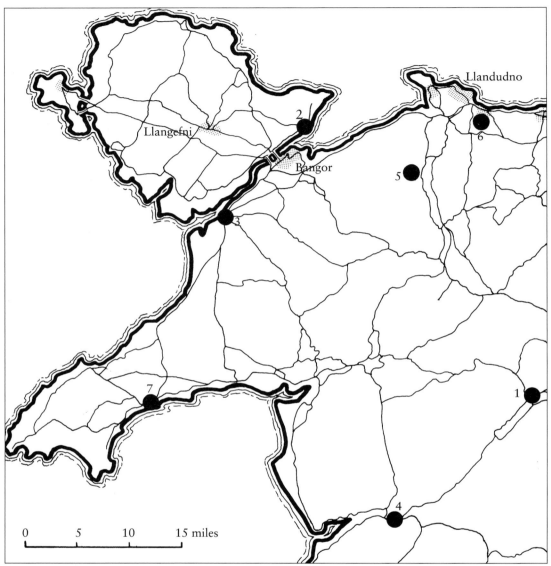

Llandudno

Llangefni

Bangor

6

5

2

3

7

1

4

0   5   10   15 miles

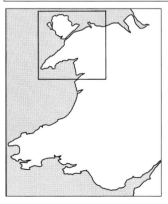

1. Bala
2. Beaumaris
3. Caernarfon
4. Dolgellau
5. Llanbedr-y-cennin
6. Llanelian-yn-Rhos
7. Pwllheli

The Old Bull, BALA

(SH 926 359)

Today Bala is a mecca for fishing and boating enthusiasts who converge on the town for an assault on Llyn Tegid, the largest natural lake in Wales. The town has been standing here since at least the fourteenth century, although the only relic of that period is Tomen y Bala castle mound at the top of the High Street. From its position on the main road from Dolgellau to Llangollen, the town was a popular stopping place for early travellers and antiquarians, although it was the lake and castle earthworks which invariably captured their attentions. Sir William Colt-Hoare was impressed with the local architecture on his visit in 1797: 'several cottages are rendered picturesque from their dilapidated state and the grass and other plants sprouting from their thatched roofs'. At that time there were only two major inns in Bala, the Old Bull and the White Lion. The latter is a large rambling whitewashed building with fake half-timbering, which locals used to boast was the best inn in Wales. George Borrow stayed here, as did Sir William, whose visit coincided with a Methodist meeting across the road. When the Methodists' vociferous enthusiasm reached fever pitch, the unfortunate traveller scurried to his diary to complain about the noise.

Just opposite the Lion stands the Old Bull, an older building with a more restrained and dignified façade. It is said to date from 1692 and was used as a coaching inn until the 1960s; the disused mounting block still survives in the rear yard. The refurbished interior has been opened out into two main bar-lounges with a more modern dining area at the rear. On the walls are photographs of old Bala, though there is no visual record of the flourishing sock trade which was the mainstay of the economy. Early travellers were fascinated and amused by the sight of men, women and children lining the roadside, busily knitting socks. In 1778 Thomas Pennant wrote: 'during Winter the females, through love of society, often assemble at one another's houses to knit, sit around a fire, and listen to some old tale, or to some ancient song, or the sound of the harp'.

Bala lies about 14 miles north-east of Dolgellau, along the A494 to Corwen. Bar snacks and meals, accommodation. Open 11 a.m.–11 p.m.

The George and Dragon, BEAUMARIS
(SH 604 760)

Beaumaris has one of the largest and most perfectly designed castles in Britain, and yet this innocuous giant slumbers in ruins at the far end of the seaside town. Lacking the dramatic setting of its near neighbours Conwy and Caernarfon, Beaumaris Castle makes up for this with a complex plan conceived to outwit the most dedicated of attackers. Unfortunately the thirteenth-century defences failed to hold back the army of Owain Glyndwr, who captured the castle and burnt the town in 1403. When order was restored the townsfolk belatedly set about enclosing the borough with masonry walls, and within the protective enclave the gutted houses were rebuilt.

Although stone is an abundant building material in North Wales, the medieval towns had a surprisingly high proportion of timber-framed buildings, though very few survive today and only antiquarian drawings record what has been lost. Aberconwy House at Conwy is a lucky survivor and is now owned by the National Trust. Here in Beaumaris the only obvious timber-framed building is a shop in Castle Street, but a much more fascinating building is the George and Dragon in Church Street. All outward signs of antiquity are hidden beneath a bland rendered façade, but once inside the lattice of blackened wood leaves no doubt that this was once a half-timbered building. The outer walls have been largely rebuilt in brick and stone, but enough remains to show that the street front had an overhanging upper floor, and at the rear there was a projecting gallery overlooking a courtyard or garden. The garden has been replaced by a kitchen, which now forms a rear seating area. On the wall of the lounge is an extract from *The Times*, dating from November 1805, recording the death of Nelson, and a collection of bank notes from all over the world. There is also a copy of John Aubrey's celebrated seventeenth-century verse:

> To save a mayd St George the Dragon slew –
> Most say there are no dragons, and 'tis sayd
> there was no St George:
> Pray God there was a mayd.

By the 1970s the George and Dragon was showing more than a few signs of age, and the landlord decided to carry out repairs to the leaky roof. As the plaster was stripped from the walls and false ceilings taken down in an upstairs room, a remarkable series of wall paintings came to light. A team

Beaumaris, George and Dragon: this reconstruction of the late sixteenth-century town house shows the main chamber in the process of being decorated in the summer of 1610. There was an oversailing jetty along the street front and, less usual, an open gallery at the rear (not visible from this angle)

from the Royal Commission on Ancient and Historical Monuments spent several days recording the paintings, and restoration work was afterwards carried out to preserve the unique design. All the vertical and diagonal beams of a partition wall had been decorated with chevrons, and the main horizontal beam of the roof truss carried Latin mottoes such as 'Peace be with you', 'Know thyself', and 'God provides'. Not all of the paintings survived their ruthless treatment in more modern times, and much of the central design is unclear. On one of the panels can be seen two horned devils' heads, and so the design may have been a representation of heaven and hell. The topmost panel certainly had a religious significance for it shows a cross and the symbols of the Passion (the wounded hands and feet of Christ). Many years ago the date 'August 1610' was seen on one of the attic timbers, and this very likely commemorates the redecoration of the house, for the building itself is older. According to tradition the inn was built in 1410 in the aftermath of the Glyndwr rebellion, but all the architectural details suggest a date in the more settled and prosperous days of Queen Elizabeth I. This was the home of a well-to-do individual, perhaps with Catholic sympathies. He was probably a wealthy merchant, for Beaumaris in the later Middle Ages was the commercial capital of North Wales – as the saying 'the lawyers of Caernarfon, the merchants of Beaumaris, and the gentry of Conwy' recalls. Beyond this we know nothing else about the person who commissioned the paintings, though it is interesting to speculate that the 'devils' could be stylized bulls' heads which form the heraldic crest of the Bulkeley family. This affluent and important family is recorded in Beaumaris in the fifteenth century, and its manor house of Hen Blas stood only a few doors along from the George and Dragon. This building also had painted beams and a beautiful Elizabethan plaster ceiling; it would have been the showpiece of the town had it evaded demolition in 1869.

The Bulkeley crest is also echoed in another historic pub here, the Bull's Head in Castle Street. It was supposedly built in the fifteenth century, although the Royal Commission date it to the seventeenth century, and the imposing façade with rows of sash windows is the result of an eighteenth-century facelift. This was the main coaching inn in Beaumaris when the town formed a link in the London to Holyhead road network. Before Telford built his suspension bridge over the Menai Straits, coach passengers would be driven across Lavan Sands to a waiting ferry opposite Beaumaris. During the Civil War the castle was held for the king by Sir Richard Bulkeley, and the parliamentary leader, General Mytton, commandeered the Bull's Head as a base for the duration of the siege. There is a story that one of his troops was found drunk in the George and court-martialled. The decor inside includes a collection of cutlasses, a seventeenth-century brass clock, and a wooden ducking stool – which is a particularly ironic memento to have in a pub, since landlords serving watered-down ale or poor measures were just as likely as gossiping women to be given a dip!

Beaumaris lies near the south-eastern end of Anglesey, signposted along the A545 from Menai Bridge. Bar snacks and meals (accommodation at the Bull's Head). Open 11 a.m.–11 p.m.

The Black Boy, CAERNARFON
(SH 478 628)

'I have travelled through many towns in England, but I have never seen so many drunkards in proportion to the number of the population, as in Caernarvon,' complained a correspondent to a local newspaper in the nineteenth century. Even as late as 1848 the punishment for persistent drunkenness was a spell in the stocks, and in defence one can only point out that there were at least fifty pubs in this comparatively small town, and so temptation was everywhere. When the Revd Mr Bingley visited Caernarfon in the early nineteenth century it was not the drunks who aroused his ire, but fellow Christians. Just as Colt-Hoare was annoyed by ebullient Methodists (p. 161), so too was Bingley, and he commented sourly that a gathering of ecstatic believers had 'more the appearance of heathen orgies than of the rational spirit of Christian devotion'.

Whatever their gripes and groans, no traveller could complain about being short-changed by the majestic castle which guards the town and harbour, and was built by Edward I in 1283. The checker-board street system has remained unchanged since the thirteenth century, and the protective belt of walls and towers built along with the castle still define and enclose the old town centre. One of the oldest surviving buildings here is the Black Boy inn, which stands in the quiet thoroughfare of Northgate Street – or 'Four and Six Street' for Welsh speakers. The unusual name is thought to recall the days when sailors in need of lodgings could have a hammock for 4*d*, or a bed for 6*d* (with female company thrown in for good measure!). There is also a puzzle concerning the name of this seventeenth-century inn; the sign outside depicts a coloured slave, but some people believe that the 'boy' in question is Edward the Black Prince or, more prosaically, a black buoy that marked the entrance to the harbour. The inn was built in several stages in the late seventeenth century, and the oldest part is the bar-lounge of the hotel wing, with its beamed ceiling and inglenook fireplace. A passage at the rear leads to the dining room and kitchens, and there is a legend (quite unfounded) that this path once led to a nunnery. The public bar is housed in an adjoining wing which also has a huge inglenook, though this one is no longer used and the stonework has been painted a garish red and black.

One other pub deserves a brief mention here, although it no longer survives, having fallen a victim to town redevelopment in the last century. The Red Lion in Palace Street was a pub only from the eighteenth century. Before then it had been Plas Pulesdon, the sumptuous residence of the medieval sheriffs of Caernarfon. Old etchings show that the building had rows of leaded windows and an overhanging upper floor; and, according to popular tradition, it was from the balcony that a Welsh mob lynched the hated sheriff Roger Pulesdon in 1295.

The town stands on the banks of the Menai straits about 7 miles south-west of Bangor, on the A487 to Porthmadog. Bar snacks and meals, accommodation. Open 11 a.m.–11 p.m.

The Stag, DOLGELLAU
(SH 728 178)

Dolgellau started life as a medieval borough on the banks of the river Wnion, but unlike nearby Bala there was no formal planning in the layout, and the town grew up beside St Mary's church like an unpruned tree. Only in recent years has traffic congestion in the tangled streets been relieved with a bypass road. The mainstay of the economy was cloth and woollen manufacture, and the prosperity of the town was boosted in the nineteenth century with the discovery of gold in the hills to the north. A few of the mines are still in operation, but at most of them only spoil heaps and gaping tunnels mark the venture. For years the town has been an important stopping place on the main north-south road, and a centre for the adventurous rambler tackling the heights of Cadair Idris. There were once dozens of pubs here catering to the needs of travellers and itinerant workers, some cottages divided into two or more 'tippling houses' – and even empty barns were used. In 1798 the Revd J. Evans and his travelling companions tried to get accommodation at one of the inns here, but unfortunately came across a landlord who believed they were good-for-nothing Irish immigrants, and whose wife suspected they were criminals on the run!

The Stag is the oldest pub in town and it stands at the bottom end of Bridge Street, where the twisting roads converge on the seventeenth-century bridge. It is now part of a terrace of similar buildings, although the Stag once stood alone, and the plain and rugged stonework so evident in this grey town is here decorously rendered. Even the interior is without its obligatory bare masonry, but the beer garden offers a glimpse of the untreated rear walls and the massive boulders which make up the Dolgellau houses. The Stag appears to date from the late seventeenth or early eighteenth century, though there are few original features visible apart from some old beams and a large, disused inglenook beside the dartboard. A few miles outside town at Rhydymaen stands the Hywel Dda inn, a popular stopping place for travellers using the busy A494 to Bala. It is not as old as the Stag, and the rugged stone walls convey an impression of great age that the comfortable and modernized interior pleasantly refutes.

The town of Dolgellau lies roughly midway between Machynlleth and Trawsfynydd on the A470. It can also be reached from Barmouth via the A496, or from Bala along the A494. Bar meals. Open 10.30 a.m.–11 p.m.

The Old Bull Inn, LLANBEDR-Y-CENNIN
(SH 761 695)

The village and church of Llanbedr-y-cennin cling precariously to the steep wooded hillside of Pen-y-gaer above the Conwy valley. There is a local tradition (of dubious veracity) that the road to the village was once so steep that horses and carts had to be helped along with a pulley and rope. Whether or not this is true, the old track through the village was in use as far back as Roman times by travellers leaving the Conwy valley and crossing Bwlch y Ddeufaen, in order to avoid the treacherous Penmaenmawr coast road. In the valley below Llanbedr stands the site of the Roman fort of Caerhun, while on the mountain top above is an Iron Age hillfort – the last stronghold of the local tribes before the imperial troops arrived.

Llanbedr-y-cennin means the church of St Peter of the leeks, though when linked with Peter's name the leek becomes a daffodil – Cennin-pedr. Neither is very common here. The village is made up of a scatter of whitewashed cottages of seventeenth-, eighteenth- and nineteenth-century date, and the Bull claims to be older than all of them. The oldest part of the inn is the long wing facing the roadside, with a painted bull adorning the gable end. There were originally three small rooms inside, but the dividing walls have come down, and there is now one long bar-lounge with stone fireplaces at either end. Narrow fortress-like windows in the thick walls offer spectacular (if restricted) views of the Conwy valley. Beyond the main inglenook a passage leads to a quiet dining area, with access to a rear wing splendidly refurbished as a restaurant.

Llanbedr-y-cennin, the Old Bull

After a drink and a meal at the pub, what could be better than an invigorating walk (weather permitting) up to the summit of Pen-y-gaer, to marvel at the views and the ingenuity of ancient man?. To stop any chariot-borne enemy sneaking up on the fort, the inhabitants lined the road with row upon row of upright stones, which can still trip up the unwary rambler today!

The village of Llanbedr can be reached off the B5106 Conwy to Betws-y-coed road. If travelling from Betws there is a signposted left-hand turn about a mile beyond Dolgarrog. Bar snacks and meals. Open 12–3 p.m. (11–3 p.m. Saturday), 7–11 pm.; closed Monday lunchtimes.

The White Lion, LLANELIAN-YN-RHOS
(SH 864 764)

A hundred years or more ago, if anyone announced that they had visited the hilltop village of Llanelian, the reply would not have been 'how nice', but 'who did you curse?' During the eighteenth and nineteenth centuries the spring

Llanelian, the White Lion: notice the change in masonry which shows that the front of the inn has undergone rebuilding

of Ffynnon Elian near the church was visited by hundreds of hate-wishers and grudge-bearers, for the waters were believed to hold dark powers. Those wishing ill on their neighbours would utter a curse and drop into the well a pebble carved with the name of the intended victim. A fee was then paid to the custodian. Whether any real misfortune befell anyone as a direct result of the supernatural threat can only be guessed at, but such was the notoriety of the well that fear and foreboding would set in once the victim had been told of what had occurred. Only by paying the custodian a higher fee could the pebble be removed, and the curse redirected. The continual cycle of pathetic and petty hates continued until the vicar blocked up the spring to stop the practice.

Had he not done so, then perhaps Llanelian would be a very popular tourist centre, though inevitably at the cost of its solitude and rural charm. A few modern buildings have sprung up, but despite its proximity to Colwyn Bay the village has changed little over the years. The fifteenth-century church of St Elian stands on the edge of a breezy hillside overlooking Colwyn and the Llandudno peninsula, and tucked into the graveyard wall is the White Lion. Few other villages can boast of such an obvious link between church and inn, for the path to the church crosses the cobbled courtyard of the Lion. The low, whitewashed building on the opposite side of the yard was originally a bakery, and a cast-iron oven door has been salvaged and set up in the bar. At one time it was also used as a schoolroom. The present owners hope to restore the dilapidated building and incorporate it into the premises.

Before entering the inn it is worth having a quick look at Llan Cottage across the road. This low, thatched building is far older than the Lion, but gives a good impression of how the pub may have once looked. The roof has been raised, slates now replace thatch, and the windows have been enlarged; but the huge lateral chimney (so obvious at Llan) still remains at the rear. Within, the bar-lounge has a large inglenook with a curving lintel, and a floor of polished flagstones, under which is said to be a deep well. At the rear an old barn has been refurbished as an attractive dining area, with some reused ceiling beams which came from a demolished chapel in Old Colwyn. Although from the outside the White Lion appears to be no earlier than the nineteenth century, the lateral fireplace and evidence of rebuilding suggests it is older – though it most certainly does not date from the eighth century as the sign claims! If you look closely at the outer frame of the bar window, you may glimpse a faint pattern of pellet holes. Several years ago a local farmer had a blazing row with the landlord and, since there was no longer any well for the traditional vengeance, returned with his gun and took a pot shot at the building. While the enraged farmer kept guard on the front door, the landlord's son escaped through the back to fetch the police.

Llanelian lies on the mountainside above Colwyn Bay, and can be reached by several signposted minor roads. The easiest is from the A55 at Colwyn; follow the B5383 to Betws for ³/₄ of a mile, and then take a right turn which climbs steeply to the village. Bar snacks and meals. Open 11 a.m.–3 p.m. (12–3 p.m. weekdays), 6–11 p.m.

Penlan Fawr, PWLLHELI
(SH 375 351)

Walking around Pwllheli today, any visitor will be hard pressed to realize that this coastal town on the arm of Lleyn started life as a medieval borough, so great has been the subsequent rebuilding. During the Glyndwr rebellion the town was razed, but the community slowly recovered and started to prosper as a port and shipbuilding centre. Dr Samuel Johnson visited the town in 1774 during a tour of north Wales, although his comments would hardly have endeared him to the locals; 'we went to Pwllheli, a mean old town'. Gripes notwithstanding, the good doctor still 'bought something to remember the place'! Since the topography of the town has changed so much it is difficult to appreciate that the inn once stood close to the water's edge, and on most evenings would have been packed with a riotous mix of sailors, smugglers and shipbuilders. We do not know if Dr Johnson braved the convivial atmosphere, though at that time there were about eight other pubs here, and the Penlan was known as the Red Lion.

As the population of the town grew, so too did the pubs, and by the 1830s there were thirty-two recorded alehouses and taverns here. The Penlan also had a wider social function; the first Wesleyan preached here in 1802, and a few years later a private school was established in a rear room. Although the inhabitants triumphed over man-made disasters, nature proved to be a more intractable enemy, and during the nineteenth century the economy suffered as the harbour began to silt up. The last ship was built here in 1878. Today the oldest building in the town is the Penlan Fawr, which dates from the first half of the seventeenth century. From the outside the building has undergone certain changes: the small windows have been opened out, a large entrance cut through the front of the imposing porch, and fake half-timbering affixed to the upper walls. But the interior is almost unaltered, so that an itinerant preacher or irascible doctor would feel quite at home. The bar-lounge has a flagstone floor and beamed ceiling, with a large inglenook in the end wall. Hidden behind the entrance passage and stairwell is a smaller, and quieter, seating area with a doorway leading to the rear games room.

Pwllheli makes an ideal centre for touring the Lleyn peninsula, though Abersoch and Criccieth are equally popular if not so centrally placed. The surrounding countryside holds a surprisingly varied heritage of ancient monuments stretching back thousands of years, from prehistoric tombs to medieval castles. More relevant to this book is the restored fifteenth-century Penarth Fawr Hall, which lies a few miles away off the Criccieth road. The spacious interior, crowned with an ornate timber roof, conveys a good impression of what pubs such as the Tram Inn (p. 83) and the Black Swan (p. 96) were like in their prime.

The Penlan stands in the street of the same name in Pwllheli town centre. Pwllheli lies on the Lleyn peninsula, and can be reached from Caernarfon via the A499, or from Porthmadog along the A497. Bar meals (lunchtimes only). Open 11 a.m.–11 p.m.

INDEX